CONSUMER PROTECTION FOR BOAT USERS

A.A.Painter

MBIM, MITSA, AIArb.

Nautical

First published 1979 in Great Britain by
NAUTICAL PUBLISHING COMPANY LIMITED
Lymington, Hampshire SO4 9BA

in association with
George G. Harrap and Company Limited
182-184 High Holborn, London WC1V 7AX

ISBN 0 245 53450 4

By the same author:
A Guide to Consumer Protection Law
The Councillor and Consumer Protection

Photoset and printed in Great Britain by
Printwise, 85b High Street, Lymington, Hampshire

CONSUMER PROTECTION FOR YACHTSMEN

Preface			6
Chapter	1	Charting a course through the law	7
	2	Defective vessels, chandlery, and fittings	11
	3	Doing business with a yard or contractor	17
	4	Making a good contract	22
	5	Buying a new yacht	29
	6	Buying a second hand yacht	37
	7	Selling a yacht	46
	8	Employing a surveyor	55
	9	Buying on credit	60
	10	Obtaining a mooring	66
	11	False trade descriptions	72
	12	When things go wrong	77
	13	Going to court	83
	14	Some case studies	90
Appendix	A	A suggested form of contract for private sales of second hand yachts	97
	B	Suggested letter of instruction to a yacht broker for the sale of a second hand yacht	99
	C	Draft letter to a retailer concerning goods which are not of merchantable quality etc.	100
	D	Draft letter for use if an unsatisfactory reply or no reply at all is received in response to a letter in the form of appendix C	101
Index			102

Preface

Why do we need a book about consumer protection for boat users? Surely sailors are rugged individualists well able to look after themselves and, after all, there are books and leaflets galore for consumers. At one time that would certainly have been my view, but after fifteen years on the water, during which I have owned four cruising yachts, spent more money than I could properly afford, and had my fair share of troubles, I can only conclude that there must be a need for a simple, straightforward book especially written for the boat owner. The fact is that the average sailor, whether he has a dinghy or a seagoing yacht, enters into thousands of contracts in a life time, and by the law of averages some of them must go wrong.

This little book is not only about the law. There are many lessons I have learned over the years which, had I heeded them myself, would have saved me some worrying problems. There is much which can be done to avoid trouble if a few basic rules are understood, if suppliers are selected carefully, and if a few elementary precautions are taken. In this book I attempt to indicate the right direction in buying everything from a shackle to an ocean racer, in selecting a broker when selling, in dealing with yards, contractors, surveyors and marinas, which together serve the needs of the amateur sailor.

I would like to express my sincere appreciation to the Ship and Boat Builders' National Federation, the Association of Brokers and Yacht Agents, and the Yacht Brokers, Designers and Surveyors Association for permission to quote from their various publications, and for all the help I have received in writing this book from the legal advisers and members of those organisations.

Chichester
March 1979

1 Charting A Course Through The Law

To everyone except lawyers the law is a mysterious thing and about as exciting as being becalmed in the rain. There is nothing to be done about that, but it is essential to have a basic idea about the nature of the law and what it is capable of doing. On the assumption that yachtsmen who are also lawyers will not have bought this book, we begin with a simple explanation of the law. What is the difference between civil and criminal law, statutes and regulations, prosecutions and actions, magistrates courts, county courts and crown courts, and so on? Without this knowledge the remedies we can seek to solve a problem will not be clear to us.

Criminal laws are those passed by the state for the protection of the population in general. If Parliament considers that a certain activity is undesirable, then it passes a law against it, and a breach of that law is a crime. Such breaches may be prosecuted in the magistrates' courts or the Crown Courts and, if proved, may be punished by a fine or imprisonment. In consumer law it is a crime to misdescribe goods sold to the public.

Civil laws are also passed by the state and they set up the rules on which disputes between two or more individuals, or companies, may be solved by the courts. If a yachtsman buys a defective item from a chandler who will do nothing about it then the buyer may sue the chandler in the county courts, and if the court finds for the yachtsman the chandler may be ordered to pay damages, or provide some other remedy to recompense the buyer. An action in the civil courts does not result in a fine or imprisonment, and actions at civil law are not recorded as convictions.

Statutes are Acts of Parliament which have been right through the Parliamentary process. They begin life as a BILL and then go through stages known as 'readings' in both Houses of Parliament, plus a committee stage during which the bill is considered in detail. After completing all stages the final bill receives the Royal Assent and becomes an Act of

Parliament. Statutes are both criminal and civil law. In consumer matters the Trade Descriptions Act and the Unfair Contract Terms Acts are both statutes, but the first is criminal law and the second is civil law.

Regulations are made by government departments under powers granted by a statute. Because it necessarily takes a long time to get an Act through the Parliamentary process and because matters of a technical and complex nature cannot be dealt with by statute it is common for Ministers of the Crown to be given such powers. The regulations so made are known as Statutory Instruments. Once regulations have been drafted it is merely necessary for them to be laid on a table in the House of Commons for a prescribed period before they are signed by the appropriate Minister and assume the full force of law. Sometimes the Regulations create an offence themselves, that is, a breach of them can be prosecuted in the courts. In other cases the regulations merely add emphasis and detail to principles created by statute. In consumer matters regulations are often used to impose requirements for the giving of essential information to consumers. The regulations which control the advertising of credit are an example. The majority of regulations relate to criminal law matters.

A Prosecution results from a breach of a criminal law and is heard, in nearly all consumer matters, by a local magistrates' court. In some serious cases under the Trade Descriptions Act, 1968, for example, it is open to the prosecutor to apply for 'indictment', that is, a trial by jury before a Crown Court, which is a superior court to a magistrates' court.

Most criminal laws restrict power to prosecute to a public authority. In consumer matters this is nearly always the Trading Standards or Consumer Protection department of a local authority, or the Office of Fair Trading. However, any citizen can bring his own prosecution under the Trade Descriptions Act 1968, and certain other statutes do not specify who shall bring a prosection, and it is therefore open to any one to do so. An example is the Unsolicited Goods and Services Act, 1971, which, amongst other things, prohibits the making of demands for payment for goods sent to consumers without an order.

It is very unusual for private citizens to bring their own prosecutions in consumer matters. The law is complex and the risk of high costs in the event of failure is daunting. As far as is known only two such cases under the Trade Descriptions Act have been brought to court in the last ten years, and both of them were lost.

An Action or Suit is brought by a private citizen or a company against another in respect of breaches of contract, faulty or misdescribed goods, debts, and many other matters. These are actions at civil law and, in consumer matters, nearly all of them take place in the local county court. All civil law cases are brought by individuals or companies. Public authorities never take such actions on behalf of others although they may, through their consumer advice service, give information about how it can be done. But under recent changes the separation of civil and criminal law has been blurred. It is now possible, indeed quite common, for local authorities to ask for an order for 'compensation' on behalf of an aggrieved purchaser at the end of a trial at criminal law. For example, a yachtsman buys a marine engine which is claimed to have a rated power output of 30 bhp and a maximum fuel consumption of 5 pints an hour; but after installation he finds that it will not develop the claimed power and has a fuel consumption greatly in excess of the claimed maximum. A false trade description has been applied to the engine, and the case may be prosecuted before the magistrates' or the Crown court by the local authority. The prosecutor may ask for a compensation order on behalf of the buyer once the court has announced that the case has been proved. We discuss the value of compensation orders in more detail in chapter 11.

It should be appreciated that where goods have been misdescribed the local authority is not obliged to take a prosecution. Their job is to protect the population as a whole, and they are not obliged to take up the cudgels on behalf of one buyer no matter how strong his case may be. There are also many cases which do not constitute an offence at criminal law, but which should be taken to a civil court. The requirements of the two branches of law are different, and the degree of proof required in criminal cases is higher.

A prosecution and civil action can often, as we have seen above, flow from the same incident. Examples are legion. A can of paint stated to contain 2 litres but holding considerably less is an offence against the Weights and Measures Act, but the buyer could sue in the county court for the value of the missing paint. A marine fitting stated to be made of 'stainless steel' but actually made from a metal of inferior quality would be deemed to have had a false trade description applied to it under the Trade Descriptions Act, but the buyer could sue under his rights at civil law on the grounds that the fitting was not of merchantable quality. A yard having completed a re-fit on a yacht and claiming to have completed work which was later proved not to have been done would commit an offence of making a reckless statement about the provision of a service under the Trade Descriptions Act, but the owner could sue for breach of contract, and so on.

We discuss all these matters in later chapters, but it is worth while to get the basic principles right at the outset. It is a common mistake to believe that the Trade Descriptions Act can do something for the buyer of defective goods or bad services. It cannot, unless as stated above, a compensation order is obtained by the prosecutor, and that is not always wise.

2 Defective Vessels, Chandlery, And Fittings

Everything a yachtsman may wish to buy is defined by law as 'goods'. Some things, such as permanent buildings, are exempted from the various legal definitions of 'goods' but it is safe for a yachtsman to think of all his requirements, from a length of line to an ocean going yacht as being 'goods'. The term is important because the remedies for defective goods differ from those for services. This latter term includes all those things normally done by a yard, a surveyor, or those who service or repair vessels and equipment and so on. Of course many services include goods too, and in such circumstances there are essentially two contracts, the overall one for service, and the supply of goods element of that service.

A contract is any agreement between two or more people to sell or buy goods or to provide a service. It need not be in writing, and every transaction, no matter how simple, is a contract. The purchase of a single wood screw is a contract in law in the same way as buying a complete yacht. Each contract imposes liabilities on the contracting parties.

A retailer is responsible in law for everything he sells. Normally we think of a shop when talking about a retailer, but in the case of boats and equipment the term can cover any person or company who supplies goods directly to the buyer. A chandler is obviously a retailer, but so too is the company which builds and supplies a complete vessel directly to the buyer. In respect of imported goods the principle is the same. If the importer supplies the goods to the buyer then he is the retailer, and must take responsibility for defects. The yachtsman who buys directly from an overseas supplier must be careful for he has no remedy under British law if something goes wrong.

Some people now believe that the law bears unduly harshly on retailers, but the principle is that the businessman is expected to know his business and is responsible for what he sells. He cannot pass off this responsibility onto a manufacturer or other person who supplied him. If he is sensible he will have covered himself by a good contract of supply with the manufacturer or wholesaler, but he cannot evade his responsibility to his customers.

A manufacturer's guarantee does not affect the relationship between a retailer and his customers. It does not remove or restrict the rights of the buyer against the retailer, but it does form a second and separate contract between the buyer and the manufacturer. It is sometimes a question of judgement as to whether it is better to insist upon one's rights under the law against the retailer, or to seek a remedy directly from the manufacturer under his guarantee. On the whole it is best to ask the retailer to put the matter right as he is obliged to do, and to inform the manufacturer in writing of the defect. The two can then sort the matter out between themselves.

When buying second hand goods great care must be taken. Although the legal protection for the buyer does apply to second hand goods bought from a dealer, the courts would take into account the reasonable life expectancy of the goods in dispute and their price. If second hand goods are bought from a private person then most of the protection of the law does not apply, and the buyer has no remedy in matters of fitness for purpose and quality. Buying at an auction or by competitive tender is also dangerous because in this situation the buyer is not considered to be a 'consumer' and his rights are greatly diminished.

It is illegal for a dealer to advertise his wares as if he were a private seller. If convicted he may be punished by a severe fine because he is misleading the buyer as to his rights at law.

The law protecting the consumer comes from four very important statutes. They are the Sale of Goods Act, 1893, the Supply of Goods (Implied Terms) Act, 1973, the Unfair Contracts Terms Act, 1977, and the Misrepresentation Act, 1967. It is as well to know about them and to be able to quote them in the event of a dispute. The basic rules are still those established by the 1893 Act. Old they may be, but they have withstood the test of time very well, and as modified and amended by later Acts they provide a copper bottomed guarantee of protection to every consumer.

All goods sold to the consumer must meet three basic requirements:-

1. The goods must correspond to the description given of them. This is an obvious requirement, but it means that anything said about the goods must be true. The rule is set by the 1893 Act, reinforced by the 1973 Act, and if any misrepresentation forms a part of the contract then that contract may be cancelled by virtue of the 1967 Act. If a radio direction finder, for example, is claimed to have an effective range of 75 miles it must have just that; 65 will not do. Rope claimed to have a breaking strain of 5 tons must live up to that claim; 4½ tons will not do. Sails claimed to have a composition of 85% terylene and 15% nylon must contain those substances in the amounts claimed. A ratio of 90% and 10% will not do even though, for all practical purposes the material may be just as good. In every case where misdescribed goods are sold the buyer can reject them and the contract is cancelled. Where a British Standard is quoted, as in the case of marine ply-wood, the detailed specification must be met.

2. Goods must be of merchantable quality. This means that they must be capable of doing what they are supposed to do, subject to the price paid for them, the description applied to them and any other circumstances relating to the contract. For example, it would be unreasonable to expect a compass costing £45 to have the same sensitivity or accuracy as one costing £150, but it must be capable of performing with an accuracy commensurate with its price. To take another example, a cheap paint brush cannot be expected to give the finish nor to last as long as an expensive brush, but it must last as long and give as good a finish as any reasonable yachtsman would expect it to. You get what you pay for in this life, and the law recognises the fact.

3. Goods must be fit for the purpose intended for them. By this we mean that where the buyer relies upon the advice of the seller in selecting something to meet his needs, the article must live up to that expectation. This is a very important rule for yachtsmen as unless the item to be bought is a simple article the properties of which are well known, or the yachtsman is very experienced, it is a wise precaution to seek the advice of the seller. Tell him what the thing is wanted for and be guided by his advice. If it should then prove to be unfit for the purpose, the yachtsman has a case. If he did not rely on the advice of the seller, or did not seek it, then he cannot expect to have a remedy at law if it fails to meet his purpose.

A simple example is the selection of a shackle for a particular job, perhaps to attach an anchor to its chain. The wise yachtsman will look up the correct size of shackle and the material of which it should be made to meet the weight of his anchor, the length of his chain, and the type of vessel concerned. If he has not done that, then he should explain his needs to the chandler and follow his advice. If too small a shackle is selected for the job without the advice of the seller having been sought, the very least will be a lost anchor. The worst could be much more serious, and the seller will not be liable, on grounds of fitness for purpose. If the shackle were of the right size and made of the right material but failed despite the fact, then the matter would be actionable on grounds of merchantable quality.

These then are the principles which the law prescribes for every consumer transaction, and if the goods bought fail any of them the remedy is clear. The retailer must refund the cost of the goods to the buyer, or he may offer a replacement, or he may offer to have the fault repaired. But the important thing to remember is that the choice rests with the buyer. The seller cannot refuse to refund the price to the buyer on the grounds that he is willing to exchange or repair defective goods. He has an absolute liability in all the circumstances outlined above to refund the price. The alternatives are up to the buyer. The seller cannot insist on a credit note being issued either, although there is nothing to prevent the buyer from accepting one if he so wishes.

Contracts work both ways however, and no buyer can insist on his money back, simply because he has changed his mind. Before any of the rights afforded to the consumer by law become available there must be a clear and unequivocal breach of one of the three principles discussed above. A moment's thought shows that this is only fair and reasonable. Trade would be impossible for retailers if consumers could demand their money back on a whim. The fact that certain very large multiple retailers do exchange goods or refund money on demand does not mean that there is any legal obligation to do so. It is a matter of commercial judgement for them. In a good contract the seller promises to supply goods properly described, fit for the purpose, and of merchantable quality, and the buyer promises to pay an agreed price for them. Both are bound by the contract, and must stand by the bargain made.

All of this is true enough in regard to simple contracts, but what about a complete yacht, for example? Would it be reasonable for the buyer to demand his money back on a £10,000 yacht because a simple deck fitting broke? In theory the answer is in the affirmative, but in practice it is very unlikely that such a hard hearted yachtsman would get away with it. We are in the realms of speculation, for the courts have seen very few cases concerning marine products. That says much for the quality of British marine products, and the integrity of British companies when trouble arises, but it is worth a brief discussion of the likely outcome of a possible court case.

The law assumes the existence of an ordinary man in the street – the man on the number 21 Clapham omnibus – as he is sometimes called, by whose standards all questions of reasonableness, unless otherwise defined by law, are judged. All courts, especially the civil courts, where cases are judged on the balance of probability, must seek to do what is reasonable, and so in the case of a broken deck fitting it is likely that a court would say that an offer by the seller to replace the fitting, even if it took a little while to get one, would be a reasonable answer to the problem. After all, the vessel would still be capable of use, and in any event the price of the fitting would form such a small part of the overall cost of the vessel that to insist upon a return of the total cost would be absurd.

Between this extreme case and that of a defective shackle or can of paint, the courts are likely to judge each case on its merits. We will discuss what should be done about defective goods where the retailer will not honour his legal obligations, or a manufacturer will not comply with the terms of his guarantee in Chapter 12, but to conclude this chapter let us take a moment to remind ourselves what the various statutes quoted on page 8 actually do for us.

The Sale of Goods Act, 1893, as splendid and precise a piece of legislation as has ever been drafted, is still the basic Act upon which lies all protection for the consumer in regard to defective goods. It prescribes the principles of compliance with description, fitness for purpose, and merchantable quality with which all goods sold to consumers must comply. However, it used to be the case that manufacturers and boat builders put 'exclusion clauses' in their contracts, invoices, guarantees and other documents which reduced the rights of the buyer. Words such as *by signing this document I hereby waive all my rights at law and substitute therefore the terms and conditions of this contract* were commonplace. In the old days the consumer was bound by any such agreement he had signed and it was frequently the case that his rights under the signed contract were significantly less advantageous to him than his rights under the Sale of Goods Act would have been.

The Supply of Goods (Implied Terms) Act, 1973 and the Unfair Contract Terms Act, 1977 changed all that. The new position is that no matter what he signs the buyer's rights under the Sale of Goods Act, 1893, as amended, cannot be taken away from him. The only point to remember is that the fitness for purpose remedy is not available if the advice of the seller has not been sought in regard to yachting equipment.

Despite the 1973 Act it was still the case until 1977 that many companies inserted 'exclusion clauses' in their contracts and guarantees, or put up notices which misled the consumer as to his rights. Although their rights were preserved many people were confused by such clauses and did not seek the solutions to their problems which the law made available to them. And so, in 1977 regulations were passed under the Fair Trading

Act, 1973 which made it a criminal offence to use such clauses punishable by a substantial fine.

The Unfair Contract Terms Act, 1977 is mainly directed at services which we discuss later, but it also concerns the protection of consumers in regard to goods by extending the principles of merchantable quality etc to goods leased or hired. This is particularly important with regard to such things as life rafts which are often hired. This Act does not apply to contracts made before 1st February 1978.

The Misrepresentation Act, 1967 is a simple little statute of great value. It states that if there is any misrepresentation in any contract by either party to the contract then the contract may be null and void, that is, it may be cancelled. Again we talk about this in more detail later, but in considering any problem about defective goods it should be read together with the 1893 and 1973 Acts.

3 Business With A Yard Or Contractor

Unless a sailor sticks to dinghies and does all his own maintenance the time will inevitably come when he must do business with a yard, marine engineer, a sail maker, or some other contractor. Launching, lifting out, laying up, re-fits, engine repairs and replacements, and many other jobs are beyond the majority of yachtsmen, for they require specialist equipment and technical know-how which must be bought. It is all a very risky business and it is not necessary to own a boat for very long before something goes wrong with a contract. This is not because the marine industry is necessarily inefficient, still less dishonest, but because by the very nature of things a boat is a complex object capable of presenting an almost infinite variety of problems, and requiring a considerable range of specialist skills to keep it in good shape. Of course there are a few rogues in the marine industry, just as there are in any other business, and there are many more contractors and yards which do not always complete a contract on time or simply overlook an essential part of the job. Another problem for the industry lies in the nature of yachtsmen themselves. They are, on the whole, a pretty independently minded lot all believing themselves, usually quite wrongly, to be embryo circumnavigators. The relationship between a marine company and its customers is a sensitive one fraught with possible pitfalls, but most of them can be avoided by approaching a contract in a business like way.

The law relating to contracts for service differs from that for the sale of goods alone. True, most contracts of service in relation to boats include a 'sale of goods' element, and the law relating to those goods is the same as that described in chapter 2. But with regard to the 'services' element, that is payment for labour, expertise and specialist equipment, the law allows the parties to the contract greater freedom to negotiate the terms of the contract than is the case with goods alone. The parties may agree to whatever conditions they wish, subject only to the overall principle that the contract should be fair and capable of being discharged. There is also a legal restriction on the use of 'disclaimers for negligence' in the Unfair Contract Terms Act, 1977.

Until this Act came into force it was very common to see clauses in contracts and notices exhibited in offices and workshops containing words such as,

All vessels and gear are repaired, worked on, moved, stored and otherwise managed and kept at the sole risk of the owner, and we and our employees accept no responsibility for loss, damage or delay whatsoever, nor for any injury or loss of life to owners or their crew whilst on our premises.

Even if a clause such as this was not specifically brought to the attention of the yachtsman when he was negotiating the contract it would be binding providing it was in the documents relating to the contract or exhibited where he could reasonably be expected to see it. Thus the yard or contractor was protected against his own negligence, and the only recourse open to the owner was to insure against possible risks. This was manifestly unfair and the Unfair Contract Terms Act, 1977 seeks to redress the balance in favour of the consumer.

With regard to injury or loss of life the new Act is absolute in its effect. No contract clauses which seek to limit the liability of a yard or contractor will have the slightest effect upon the right of the owner, or in the event of his death, his dependents to seek redress against the yard for their negligence. Fortunately death or serious injury to yachtsmen because of the negligence of yards is rare, but it is obviously possible that an engine failure in a crisis situation could cause loss of life or injury, as could some defect in the hull such as a badly fitted skin fitting. There are many other examples where a yard could find itself in severe difficulties because of bad workmanship or accidents involving customers on their premises.

With regard to the loss of, or damage to, vessels and equipment the Act permits the use of disclaimers in contracts providing they are reasonable. As to what is reasonable one can only hazard a guess until cases are heard in the courts, but the Act does give some guidance. For example, if there are circumstances about the contract where possible difficulties are known, or could reasonably be expected to be known to both parties then it would be reasonable for the contractor to rely on a disclaimer in that regard. Many jobs, especially on vessels of unusual construction, reveal unexpected problems and the likelihood of their occurring ought to be known to both the yard and the owner. In some cases it is known that owners insist on a job being done in a certain way, or using certain materials, against the advice of the contractor. In such a case it would be reasonable for the contractor to protect himself by the insertion of a disclaimer clause in the contract.

Another matter which the Act requires to be taken into account is the strength of the bargaining position of the two parties to a contract. It is not always the case that the customer is in the weakest position. A wealthy yachtsman taking his vessel to a small yard in which he may have some other business advantage would hardly be regarded as being the weaker party to a contract. The courts would also be influenced by any inducement which had been offered to the yachtsman by the yard and whether he accepted it in return for the use of a disclaimer in the contract.

All in all, therefore, the Act has brought about a great improvement in the position of a yachtsman who finds himself in dispute over a contract on his yacht, but the Act does not remove the need for vigilance, and some basic precautions when entering into a contract.

There was a time when the making of a contract was a very informal affair. Many yachtsmen used to phone the yard foreman and tell him what to do. Such conversations as, "Oh Fred, would you get *Sundowner* ready for launching in early April please? I think we had better paint her topsides this year, and she needs her bottom scraped and anti-fouled. Oh yes, I think there is a leak around the stern tube – but have a good look around and do what you think necessary".

Countless thousands of contracts have been made like this over the years, and many still are. If there has been a long standing relationship between an owner and a small one man yard then fair enough, but the industry is changing rapidly as are its customers. Although there are still more than 500 firms in the business with an annual turnover of less than £100,000, the fact is that there are now a great many vessels on the water in the hands of relatively unknowledgeable owners, who are obliged to do business with limited companies through paid employees. The yachtsman seldom sees or even knows the owners of the yard. Furthermore, the period of rapid inflation in recent years and the fiscal policies of an uncaring or hostile government has caused many small companies to go to the wall or adopt a more business like way of conducting their affairs in order to survive. It is therefore clear that an entirely new contractual position has developed.

The owner who now phones a yard with vague instructions about a job is really writing a blank cheque for the yard owners. This is not to say that they are dishonest, but they are in business to make money and they can hardly be blamed for ensuring that their work is profitable to them. Many wealthy owners are perfectly happy to continue in this way – that is for them to decide – but if they do get into trouble they have little or no protection at law. For the majority of owners who sail to a budget, such a practice is foolhardy in the extreme.

Fortunately as the business has grown to meet the amazing increase in demand in recent years it has also become better organised. Nearly all good yards belong to the Ship and Boat Builders National Federation, and this trade association deserves much credit for bringing order into the industry and promoting good basic rules of business which are fair to member companies and their customers. It is always a good plan to check whether a yard is a member of the SBBNF and, if possible, to do business with a member company. That is not to say that there are no good firms outside the federation, for there are; still less is it true that all member companies are whiter than white, for like all groups of individuals or companies some are better than others. But it is true to say that the chances of entering into a bad contract are greatly reduced if business is done with a member of the SBBNF.

The SBBNF Terms of Business which are frequently updated, are used by most member companies, and many more who are not members. Usually they appear on the back of order forms which are the basis of a contract between the boat owner and the yard. Often they are exhibited in the office or the yard or, on occasions, in the workshops too. The terms of business have been carefully examined by lawyers acting for the federation, and have also been the subject of comment by those with an interest in yachting from the consumer's point of view. For normal contracts the yachtsman who enters into a contract based upon the standard terms of business of the SBBNF members is safe in that he preserves his rights under the Sale of Goods Act, 1893, as amended, the Unfair Contract Terms Act, 1977, and all other relevant consumer legislation. Of course, there are contracts where the standard terms may be inappropriate, and there is nothing to prevent any boat owner or yard from negotiating a special contract to suit their purpose. Side by side with their terms of business the SBBNF publishes an excellent guide for member companies on their liability for goods and services under consumer law.

The golden rule when entering into a contract is to put it in writing. Of course this is impracticable and unnecessary when buying a simple item over the counter, but in any other case it is vital. This is especially so in regard to contracts of service with yards, for verbal agreements are very difficult to enforce in the courts if something should go wrong. Usually it is one man's word against another, and since cases in civil law are decided on the balance of probability, the courts cannot be blamed for dismissing cases where there is no clear evidence as to liability. It is wise, when seeking a contract of service to write to the yard asking for a quotation to complete the work listed in a letter. On receipt of the quotation, assuming it to be acceptable, written confirmation that the work may proceed in accordance with the terms stated in the quotation should be given. If something should then go wrong there is written evidence on which a court may reach a decision.

4 Making A Good Contract

In order to illustrate the way in which a good and enforceable contract may be made, let us look in a little more detail at some of the clauses of the SBBNF Terms of Business. We must remember throughout that these are merely recommended to member companies. There are many other forms of contract in use, most of which are less beneficial to the yachtsman. For the purpose of this chapter we ignore the clauses relating to moorings which we will deal with in more detail in Chapter 10.

GENERAL TERMS
1. We and our employees accept no responsibility for loss, damage or delay arising from any cause whatsoever unless such loss, damage or delay was caused by, or resulted from, our negligence or deliberate act or that of those for whom we are responsible. Subject to this exception, all vessels and gear are repaired, worked on, moved, stored or otherwise managed and kept at the sole risk of the owner. Customers should therefore ensure that their vessels and/or property are adequately insured against all risks; they should also ensure that they are themselves adequately insured against third party risks as they may be liable for damage caused by their vessels, themselves or their crew whilst on or about the premises.

At first sight this clause seems very similar to that mentioned in Chapter 3 (page 18) and so it is, but it does not seek to avoid liability for negligence by the company or its employees and sub-contractors as the former one did. It therefore complies with the requirements of the Unfair Contract Terms Act, 1977. Indeed, it probably goes rather further than the Act requires for it acknowledges liability for all loss resulting from negligence whereas the Act confines total liability to injury or loss of life.

The advice to customers about insurance is prudent, and owners should check that their policies cover them for the sort of risks mentioned before leaving vessels at yards.

2. All persons using any part of our premises and/or facilities for whatever purpose and whether by invitation or otherwise do so at their own risk, unless any injury or damage to persons or property sustained within the premises and/or facilities was caused by, or resulted from, our negligence or deliberate act or that of those for whom we are responsible.

Again this clause is not contrary to the 1977 Act. The absolute liability of the contractor for loss of life or injury arising from negligence is acknowledged. The clause is also beneficial in that it clarifies the position of sub-contractors who may be engaged by the yard to complete work on a customer's vessel. The liability of the principal contractor for the negligence of sub-contractors has been a source of difficulty in the past, and the final phrase of the clause removes that difficulty.

3. Subject to express agreement to the contrary any delivery date quoted is given in good faith and is not guaranteed, but delivery shall be within a reasonable time of any date specified, bearing in mind all the circumstances of the particular case.

The marine industry has a reputation for failing to meet delivery dates which, on the whole, is richly deserved. Indeed, many experienced yachtsmen cannot remember a single contract which has been completed on time. The reasons are many and varied, because it is an industry which relies on a large number of sub-contractors, is subject to very great seasonal fluctuations in demand, is short of skilled staff, is obliged to deal with yachtsmen who are notorious for changing their minds and making last minute demands and is even, from time to time, dependent upon the weather and tides. The inability to keep to promised dates is endemic in the industry, and that being so the clause is reasonable. However, if a definite delivery date is important then it should be negotiated separately and written into the contract omitting the above clause. Reliance on the standard terms of business obliges the yachtsman to accept delivery within a 'reasonable time' of the quoted date. As to what is reasonable only a court can decide and it would be guided by all the variables we have mentioned.

4. Subject to express agreement in writing to the contrary all quotations given by us are subject to the cost of labour and materials remaining at the same level as those prevailing at the time of the quotation, and the quoted price shall be increased or decreased by the amount by which the actual cost of labour, materials and overheads has increased or decreased by reason of variation of the aforesaid levels since the date of the quotation. However, the quotation shall not be adjusted to meet increased costs which would not have occurred but for our failure to proceed with the work with reasonable despatch.

The first part of this clause is all important, for there are two ways of approaching the cost of contracts. First, there is much to be said for the negotiation of a fixed price contract, the cost of which cannot alter whatever circumstances might arise after it is signed. The boat owner then knows precisely what his commitment is, and such contracts are very common for simple jobs such as lifting out and shoring up where the time between signing the contract and its completion is small. But in longer term contracts, such as a major re-fit lasting over months, it may be that the contractor is obliged to seek a price sufficiently high to cover all eventualities. This situation, in the final outcome, may prove to be detrimental to the owner. Inflation ravages all of us, but the marine industries suffer more than most because of the relatively long time scale of business contracts, and the high cost of fittings. Whether to seek a fixed price contract or to rely upon a contract based on the SBBNF terms of business is a fine balance of judgement for the boat owner.

> *5. Quotations cover only the work and/or items specified thereon, and all additions, alterations, waiting time and any additional costs due to modified instructions will be charged to the customer at ruling prices. If in the course of executing any work we find any defect in a vessel and/or its gear that in our opinion should be rectified without delay, and before the owner's consent can be obtained, we reserve the right to carry out such necessary repair at our discretion and to charge same to the owner. Notice of any such rectification will be forwarded to the owner forthwith.*

The first part of this clause is obviously fair enough, but the second could be troublesome in the hands of an unscrupulous or inefficient yard. On the other hand it must be acknowledged that a yard should be free to take all necessary action to deal with emergency problems for failure to do so could result in liability for negligence. Unless a vessel is afloat and in danger of sinking or sustaining some other damage, it is difficult to envisage circumstances where work could be so urgent that it must be done before the owner's consent can be obtained. It is wise, unless the yard is very well known to the owner and he has absolute confidence in them to ensure that a telephone number is held by the yard at which the owner can be reached at short notice, and it is clearly understood just what can be done without prior consent. The arrangements for contact by telephone should be given to the yard in writing and a copy should be kept.

> *6. Save as provided for business customers all goods are supplied with the benefit of the appropriate undertakings (particularly as to conformity of goods with description or sample), and as to their quality or fitness by the Sale of Goods Act, 1893 as amended. Nothing in these terms shall affect those statutory rights.*

This is merely a recognition of the legal obligations of the yard to its customers. Nevertheless, it is a good thing to see it stated clearly in the contract, for it would prove that the yard was aware of the legal rights of the customer at the outset. The reference to business customers does not affect the rights of the private yachtsman. It is inserted to differentiate between the absolute protection for consumers and the qualified protection for people in the trade doing business with each other.

> 7. *Acceptance by us of goods (including vessels and/or their engines, gear, and equipment) for repair or other treatment or for mooring or storage is subject to the provisions of the Torts (Interference with Goods) Act, 1977, which confers on us as bailees a right of sale exercisable in certain circumstances. Such sale would not take place until we have given notice to the owner in accordance with the Act.*
>
> *For the purposes of the Act it is hereby recorded that:*
>
> *(a) goods for repair or other treatment are accepted by us on the terms that the owner will take delivery of the goods (at our yard or in the water adjacent thereto unless there is any written agreement or arrangement to the contrary) when the repair or other treatment has been carried out;*
>
> *(b) our obligation as custodian of goods accepted for mooring or for storage ends upon the expiry or lawful termination of the grant to the owner of facilities for mooring or storage.*

This clause is put into the terms of business to deal with the problem of goods left on the premises of a yard or contractor and not collected by the owner within a reasonable time. It is a very common problem in the marine industry because impecunious yachtsmen are inclined to leave their vessels and equipment lying around in the yard until they can raise the cash to pay for work done. From the point of view of the yard that can be a most inconvenient and troublesome problem. This clause draws the attention of customers to the rights of the company under the Torts (Interference with Goods) Act, 1977 and lays down two basic rules to be observed in any disputes which may arise. The insertion of these two points does not contravene the rights of the consumer.

A 'tort' is legal jargon for a breach of any duty required by law, and having said that it can be forgotten for the purposes of this chapter. We are discussing here the right of the yard to sell the property of a boat owner who does not collect it on time. The law has always allowed this to be done but the 1977 Act prescribes certain rules to prevent the abuse of this right. At any time after the goods are ready for collection the yard can issue a notice to the owner – it could be a letter or a formal notice. It must be sent by registered post or recorded delivery. The letter or notice must state the name of the owner and the name of the yard or contractor, and identify the goods, stating where they are being held. It must state the amount due to the yard, and the date it is proposed to sell the goods to recover the amount due. The date of the sale must be at least three months ahead of the issue of the letter or notice, and must also give the owner a reasonable opportunity of taking delivery. If there is a dispute in progress over the contract, such as one about whether the work was properly completed, then the letter or notice may not be legally issued until that dispute has been settled.

However, the courts would not take kindly to the invention of a spurious dispute by the owner in an attempt to forstall the issue of a letter or notice by the yard. It would have to be shown that the dispute existed before the question of collection of the goods arose.

Where the owner cannot be traced, the yard must still go through the motions of issuing the letter or notice to the last known address of the owner.

Once a valid notice has been given, and the time of sale has passed, the yard may sell the goods, and the new buyer becomes the legal owner. The yard can then defray whatever is owing to them out of the proceeds of the sale, including any costs incurred in arranging the sale, but must account to the customer for any amount remaining in their hands if he should subsequently appear to claim his goods. The yard is only entitled to keep the extra cash after six years have elapsed.

The purpose of this clause in the SBBNF terms of business is merely to draw the attention of customers to their rights under the Act, to stipulate that in the absence of any agreement to the contrary delivery will be at the yard or in the adjacent water, and to make it clear that the responsibility of the yard to care for goods stored or moored on their premises expires when the facilities for such storage or mooring expires or are lawfully terminated.

These rights of the yard should not be confused with the right of general 'lien' upon vessels or goods which is dealt with under the SBBNF terms of business as follows:-

> 8. Subject to any agreement to the contrary, we have the right to exercise a general lien upon any vessel and/or its gear and equipment whilst in or upon our premises or afloat at any of our moorings, until such time as any moneys due to us from the owner in respect of such vessel and/or its gear whether on account of storage or mooring charges, work done or otherwise shall be paid.

To put a general lien on a vessel merely means that it cannot be removed until debts existing on it are discharged. It does not mean that the vessel can be sold since the debts may subsequently be cleared and the obligations under the Torts (Interference with Goods) Act, 1977 would then be discharged. The lien is merely a holding exercise to prevent debtor owners from escaping their obligations.

It should also be noted that the SBBNF Terms of Business allow for minor disputes to be submitted to an informal arbitration procedure. (See Chapter 12).

SPECIFIC TERMS

So far we have discussed only the **general terms** of business relative to a contract. Important though they are, they will not prevent difficulties from arising unless the **specific terms** of the contract are clearly defined. Thus it is important that written instructions be given to every yard or contractor for every job to be done, and a copy of those instructions must be retained. The usual procedure, of course, is for an owner to go to the yard of his choice, discuss the job to be done, and then to receive a written statement of the work, together with a copy of the SBBNF terms of business. It is then for the owner to agree and allow the work to begin, or to first suggest amendments. Such an arrangement is perfectly proper and constitutes an enforceable contract for both parties. But this is not always the case. There are still a great many yards where good business practice is not established, and a loose word of mouth contract is the general rule. The owner is sometimes inclined to do business in this way in the belief that he is getting a cheaper job than he would have been able to obtain from a more businesslike yard. That may be the case on occasions, but in general it is preferable to deal with a well organised company. In any event, the precise terms of the contract should be committed to writing either by the yard or the owner.

Let us take a simple example to illustrate the point. A contract worded – *In accordance with our discussion this afternoon, I would be obliged if you would fit a new Stuart Turner 8hp engine to my sloop 'Wagtail' as soon as possible.* Even if that contract were subsequently confirmed in writing by the yard with the SBBNF terms of business appended, it would be a bad contract for it would leave too many questions unanswered and too many potential points of conflict. On the assumption that the owner has discussed the job with the yard and is aware of the work needed, a better contract would be:-

> *Following our discussions this afternoon I would be pleased to receive your quotation for the fitting of a new engine to my 23 foot sloop 'Wagtail' as follows:- Remove existing Bloggs Badstart engine and dispose of at highest value obtainable, crediting cash received therefrom to my account. Replace existing engine bearers with new in oak to accomodate new*

engine.
Install new Stuart Turner 8hp engine.
Fit new stern gear, cooling system, and sea cocks.
Fit new Muffler type exhaust system.
Install new 12 volt 45 AH Exide battery, fuse box, and associated wiring.

On receipt of the quotation, assuming it to be acceptable, a written reply should be sent as follows:-

Thank you for your quotation of the 4th July for the fitting of a new engine to my sloop 'Wagtail'. I would be grateful if you would now proceed with the work specified in my letter of the 26th June at the price quoted. I would like to take delivery of 'Wagtail' with the work duly completed on or about the 1st October next.

If the yard replies in writing that it accepts the contract then all is well. It may be that there would still be a contract in existence even if they proceeded with the work without a formal reply, but it is safer to ask them to reply in writing. Of course it may be that the yard would not be willing to accept such a closely worded contract. They may, for perfectly good reasons, have doubts about problems which could be revealed when the old engine was removed, and would wish to have some freedom of action to make good damage or weakness to the hull before completing the work. No good yard would be happy to install a new engine unless free to remedy such problems. These are matters to be negotiated before the contract is settled, or by amendment to the original contract when the problem is discovered. The terms of a contract can be varied at any time providing both parties agree to the variations. Any agreed alteration to a contract should be put into writing and formally agreed by both parties.

A final word about yards. Beware of the firm which will not enter into a well established contract. Rogues do not care to be tied to a good contract and inefficient companies are nervous of them. Furthermore, nothing which has been said in this chapter should give the impression that all big yards with impressive offices and workshops are reliable. Membership of the SBBNF includes both large and small companies, and there are many small yards which, for certain types of work, are to be preferred to the big ones.

5 Buying A New Yacht

A ready made boat off the shelf comes with all the protection given by the law which we discussed in chapter 2. A boat is no different in this regard from any other object, and the normal requirements about misrepresentation, fitness for purpose, merchantable quality, and conformity to description apply. This is also the case with larger vessels, but when ordering a new yacht to be built we introduce a different set of circumstances into the contract. For one thing we are almost certain to have to pay money to the builder as a deposit with the order, perhaps 10%, and then one or more 'building payments' during construction of the vessel, with a final payment on delivery. Thus most of the purchase price will have been paid before delivery and before the buyer has a chance to check whether the tests of fitness for purpose and so on, have been met. It is therefore obvious that the contract for the construction of a new craft is of paramount importance, as those unfortunates who have ordered a new yacht only to find that the builder has gone bankrupt before delivery have found to their cost.

Once again we turn to the SBBNF terms of Agreement, but this time to their recommended 'Agreement for the Construction of a new Craft', which has the approval of the Royal Yachting Association. There are many forms of agreement for this purpose, but we use the SBBNF version because no better form of contract for a new vessel is known to the author. There are some which are as good, achieving the same objectives with different wording, and there are others which are less praiseworthy. Any yachtsman ordering a new vessel would be well advised to insist on a contract in the form recommended by the SBBNF even if it is not that normally used by the builder. There are few builders who would risk the loss of a sale by insisting on the use of their own form of contract against one that has been produced by the SBBNF and approved by the most respected and authoritative yachting association in the world.

Identification of the contract must be beyond dispute. It should be numbered, and the full names and addresses of both parties to the contract should be stated on the front cover or at the top of the first page.

The total purchase price of the completed vessel should next appear, and this at once raises the difficult problem of value added tax. Ideally the price stated should be inclusive of VAT, but since the building of a yacht takes a considerable time it is always possible that the government may change the rate of VAT before the final payment is made. This actually happened in 1975 and caused great difficulties for builders and buyers alike. Although recommendations have been made by the Director General of Fair Trading to the government that all prices quoted for all goods should be VAT inclusive, no regulations have been made at the time of writing (1979) and it is therefore perfectly proper for builders to quote a price VAT exclusive. However, unless it is made quite clear in the contract whether VAT is included in the price or not, the buyer should insist that it is written in. It can be painful suddenly to have to find a further £1,000 or more for VAT when about to take delivery.

Building instalments are required by most yacht builders except in the case of small mass produced craft where there is sufficiently high turnover to guarantee a ready cash flow for the company. It is unlikely that even very large builders of cruising or racing vessels will ever do away with the need for staged payment, for the capital costs involved are high. The number and size of building instalments will vary according to factors such as the size, type, and total cost of the vessel, what items (perhaps including the hull) are to be bought in, the size of the building company, and so on. In the case of one very well known and successful company there are only three, that is a small deposit on order, 50% when the hull is completed, and the remaider on full completion. But the more usual arrangement is for four payments and the SBBNF recommendations are:-

1. On signing the order not more than 20% of the total price except that it should not be more than 30% in cases where the builder is buying the hull or ordering engines at an early stage.

2. Upon the hull being available at the builder's premises fully moulded, planked, plated, or formed. The SBBNF make no recommendation about the size of this payment at this stage, but it often brings up the total paid so far to 40 or 50% of the final price.

3. Upon substantial completion of the fitting of the interior joinery work, installation of the engine, or stepping of the mast, whichever is the earlier. Again the SBBNF do not recommend a percentage at this stage, but the total

payments so far are often made up to 80 or 90% of the final price.

4. Upon completion of the acceptance trials and the signing of a satisfaction note by the buyer or his agent the last payment should not be less than 10% of the total price.

Buyers should beware of any contract which does not leave ten per cent of the final payment as an absolute minimum to be paid at the conclusion of the trials, and the signing of the acceptance note. A more satisfactory amount would be 15 or 20%. This is because in the case of a dispute over the vessel that buyer has more leverage against the builder for satisfactory completion when he still owes a significant amount. It may be that the builder has a full order book and may be less than diligent in completing the contract if he has almost all of the purchase price in his pocket.

The danger of bankruptcy of the builder is always a source of concern to the buyer of a new yacht. The large number of builders going out of business in the late 1960's and early 70's resulted in a number of yachtsmen losing most of the money they had paid in building instalments, because once the company went into liquidation all the assets were taken over by the liquidator and the buyer of the uncompleted boat merely became a creditor of the bankrupt company. Such unfortunates were sometimes paid off at the rate of 10p in the £. Happily this problem is not as serious as it used to be, for the SBBNF has prudently inserted a most important clause in its recommended form of contract. It reads:-

The craft and/or all materials and equipment purchased or appropriated from time to time by the builders specifically for its construction (whether in their premises, water, or elsewhere) shall become the property of the purchaser upon payment of the first instalment under this agreement or (if it be later) upon the date of the said purchase or appropriation. The Builders shall, however, have a lien upon the craft, materials and equipment for recovery of all sums due (whether invoiced or not) under the terms of this agreement or any variation or modification thereof. Any materials or equipment rejected by the purchaser shall forthwith re-vest in the builders.

This clause means that as work progresses, and after the first payment has been made, the vessel and all materials and equipment specifically allocated to it become the legal property of the buyer, and in the event of bankruptcy before the vessel is complete the buyer would be able to remove the vessel and have her completed elsewhere. Valuable though this protection is, it does depend upon materials and equipment actually being appropriated for the contract. The fact that an engine, for example, of the type to be installed, is on the premises does not necessarily mean that it has been appropriated to the yacht in question. It may be intended for another contract. It is therefore necessary for the buyer to ensure, preferably by visiting the yard and checking on progress as building instalments are made, that the value of the yacht as she stands, together with any equipment clearly marked for installation in her, is roughly equal to the money he has paid to the builder. If it is impossible for the owner to make such visits himself, or if he lacks the knowledge to protect himself in this way it would be wise to consider employing a surveyor to do it for him.

There is one cause for concern in this matter. It may be that the yard has not paid for certain proprietary items which are on the premises and assigned to the yacht. In a recent court case it was decided that the supplier of proprietary items may have a retention of title, which means that equipment such as engines, electronic mechanisms, and the many other things bought from manufacturers for the building of a yacht will only pass to the owner if the builder has actually paid for them out of the money received in building stage payments. The position is by no means clear at the time of writing, but it does give cause for concern.

Much depends on the status of the builder. Fortunately we seem to have passed through the period where many 'get rich quickly' entrepreneurs entered the boating industry, and there are now many very good and well established builders producing attractive yachts. Nevertheless, before committing a huge sum of money to a new yacht a few enquiries about the solvency of the builder are prudent. The buyer should enquire whether the builder maintains a separate and properly designated clients' account at his bank into which all clients' monies by way of deposits or instalments are paid. Depending on the circumstances such an arrangement can reduce the buyer's risk of loss if the builder becomes insolvent.

Inflation presents a problem for the builder and buyer alike. Clearly, where the building of a new vessel is likely to last over a period of months, price rises which are often impossible to anticipate since they come from suppliers of fittings and materials, will be such that a fixed price contract for a new yacht is impossible. In the case of some very large builders who have developed almost mass production methods of building the period between order and delivery is short, and since large stocks of fittings and materials are held it is possible for them to sell by fixed price contracts. But in most cases the builder must obviously be free to increase the originally agreed price to cover inflation occurring during the period of building. The SBBNF recommended contract takes account of this factor and allows increases in building payments, in accordance with the Index of Retail Prices, on all but the first payment. Furthermore, the builder may require the purchaser to meet increased costs resulting from legislation occurring between the date of the agreement and the final instalment falling due. The contract does not allow for increased costs to be recovered from the buyer where they can be accounted for through delays in completion of the vessel for which the builder is to blame. The builder is not obliged to levy increased costs on each building payment; he can wait until the final payment and charge the whole amount at that stage. In times of high inflation the buyer is obviously in a difficult position if he is working to a strict budget for his new vessel, and the habit of some equipment manufacturers of applying price increases in the form of infrequent and therefore large amounts can add to his discomfiture. These problems can be reduced however, by sensible discussions with the builder at the point of signing the agreement. Beware of the builder who uses a contract which allows him to increase the price, but does not contain the limiting factor of the Index of Retail Prices.

Where a fixed price contract is agreed it is essential that the price variation clause is deleted from the contract.

If the buyer is late in making his payments the builder may, after a period of 28 days from giving notice that the payment is due, begin to charge interest at the rate of 3% above the Bank of England's minimum lending rate in force at the time. After a further period of 28 days the builder may sell the vessel as she lies, or complete her and sell her, unless the money is paid. After such sale the original intended buyer may recover instalments previously paid, less any loss suffered by the builder on resale. Clearly every yachtsman ordering a new vessel should ensure that he has adequate funds available to meet the building payments when they fall due within 28 days of notice from the builder. It is not unknown for over eager buyers to sign contracts believing that they can raise the money when it falls due, only to find that the government has introduced a credit squeeze and the bank manager is less sympathetic than expected.

Free and easy access to the craft during building is important, for the degree of protection for the buyer enshrined in the contract depends upon it. The SBBNF contract requires builders to permit this, subject to certain limitations designed to protect the builder against the thoroughly unreasonable buyer. The SBBNF wording on this point has been amended in the light of a recent High Court decision.

If the builder fails to proceed with the construction of the yacht without reasonable cause and in reasonable time then the buyer may, under the SBBNF contract, remove the vessel and materials and equipment appropriated to it, providing all the payments due to that date have been made. If the vessel is at a stage of construction where it is impracticable to remove it then the buyer may employ alternative labour and materials to proceed with the construction with a right of access to the builder's premises for that purpose. This protection is valuable and if the builder is going out of business, may well be capable of being invoked. But it does not require very much imagination to ponder the problems of removing a vessel, still less bringing in outside labour, if the builder is simply lazy. It is much better to make some enquiries about the efficiency of the builder before signing the contract.

It is unlikely that the courts would consider a builder to be in breach of the contract on grounds of not proceeding without reasonable cause, if he were faced with industrial action by his workers. Fortunately the marine industries are not beset by industrial problems as are many others, but it is entirely possible that a strike may delay the delivery of a yacht for many weeks or even months. If the employer could not be deemed to be prolonging the strike by unreasonable action, or lack of will to resolve it, then it is likely that the buyer would have to grin and bear it until the strike was over.

Acceptance trials on new yachts are important and the SBBNF contract includes valuable safeguards for the buyer. Briefly the contract requires the buyer, on receipt of notice that the vessel will be ready for acceptance trials by a stated date, to attend himself, or to send an agent, within 7 days following that date, to accompany representatives of the builders on trials lasting not more than a period of time stipulated in the contract. The duration will obviously vary according to the type of vessel and it is included in the contract when originally signed. If the buyer or his agent does not attend for the trials within the 7 day period, then the trials are deemed to have been held. However, the builder would, despite the contract, be expected to behave reasonably in the event of illness or other unforseen difficulties for the buyer.

If faults are found in the vessel during the acceptance trials then the contract requires the builder to correct them and the buyer may refuse to accept the vessel until this is done. After the acceptance trials have been satisfactorily completed, the buyer or his agent must sign the acceptance note, and the final payment becomes due.

But the signing of the acceptance note does not mean that further faults which may arise are the responsibility of the buyer. The normal statutory rights of the buyer under Sale of Goods law still apply and the principles of merchantable quality, fitness for purpose, and compliance with description, discussed in chapter 2, are available to the buyer. The SBBNF contract states this in unequivocal terms.

Disputes arising under a contract for a new vessel may be resolved by the normal civil courts, but the SBBNF contract contains a clause requiring such disputes to be submitted to a single arbitrator appointed by agreement between the parties to the dispute. If such agreement is not possible, then the arbitrator is appointed by the President of the SBBNF and the Chairman of the Council of the Royal Yachting Association. Arbitration is a well established method of resolving disputes under marine contracts and the system is controlled by the Arbitration Act, 1950. Arbitrators are professionally trained and carry after their names the letters FIArb., or AIArb.

Insurance of new vessels is covered by the builder up to the point where the acceptance note is signed, at which point ownership is deemed to have passed to the buyer and he becomes liable. It is therefore important for the new owner to have arranged comprehensive cover to take effect immediately after the signing of the note. If the buyer transfers some of his own equipment to the yacht before the contract is complete he must make his own arrangements for its insurance.

Delay by the builder resulting in failure to meet delivery dates can sometimes give rise to a claim for damages. But the buyer has to prove the amount of his financial loss and there is obviously room for argument as to whether delay was caused by circumstances outside the builder's control. For cases where the delivery date is of great importance to the buyer, the SBBNF has available an "agreed damages clause" which provides for an agreed rate of damages to be paid for each week of delay, subject to the buyer not exercising his right of removal or completion by outside labour. The agreed rate should, at the very least, provide a sum equal to the interest which could have been earned during the delay on the money already paid to the builder.

Buying a new yacht is an exciting period in the life of any yachtsman, and it can be a time of eager anticipation and considerable pleasure, or a positive nightmare. No contract can replace the need for the buyer to do his own research into the solvency, efficiency, and reliability of the builder. It is always wise to do business with a company which is a member of the SBBNF or, at the very least, uses a contract similar to that recommended by them.

Commissioning the building of a yacht outside the United Kingdom involves certain additional risks. Unless the buyer is prepared to instruct lawyers resident in the country concerned and to institute litigation in the courts of that country, his rights are reduced to nothing. Legal process cannot be invoked in British courts in respect of contracts outside this country. If on the other hand, the contract is negotiated with a distributor in the United Kingdom who is resident here and has assets in the UK then it would be possible to sue him. It is also worth remembering that no other country in the world has developed consumer protection law to the same extent as Great Britain.

Casting objectivity aside for a moment the author would assert that there is little point in buying foreign marine equipment or yachts unless they are of a very unique kind. The fact is that the British marine industries are supreme, and produce a range of quality of products which cannot be rivalled anywhere in the world.

6 Buying A Second Hand Yacht

The purchase of a second hand yacht can be a very risky business, especially for an inexperienced yachtsman. If the vessel to be bought is very small and cheap perhaps some degree of risk is worthwhile, especially in the case of a real bargain. But in most cases the buying of a yacht is a very significant step to take, and in terms of capital outlay, investment value, and complexity of purchase, it is second only to buying a house. Indeed, many yachts cost a good deal more than a house, and it is therefore wise to proceed very carefully. No sensible buyer would purchase a house without the help and support of a solicitor, surveyor and, perhaps, a mortgage broker, so why take unnecessary risks with a yacht?

The safeguards of merchantable quality and fitness for purpose which we discussed in chapter 2 do not apply to private sales of second hand boats. There is much discussion amongst lawyers as to how far this restricts the rights of the buyers, because the law does apply to second hand boats bought from someone selling in the course of a trade or business. For example, is a professional fisherman who sells his boat doing so in the course of his trade, or since the sale of his boat is only ancillary to his main function of catching fish, would he be regarded as a private seller? It is also the case that more and more yachts are being bought by companies either for the use of senior executives, or as part of a staff sports facility. This question has not yet been tested in the courts, but for all practical purposes it is safe to assume that unless a boat is bought from a dealer, then the valuable consumer protection contained in the Sale of Goods Act, 1893, and the Supply of Goods (Implied Terms) Act, 1973 may not be available to the buyer. However, the Misrepresentation Act, 1967 is applicable, as we shall see.

The law gives no protection to the buyer of a defective vessel from a private seller unless there has been some misrepresentation, and since the vast majority of second hand boats, even when bought with the help of a broker, are bought from private vendors this is an important matter. Although there are a few dealers in second hand boats, the sale of boats by 'trade-in' has not developed, and it is unlikely to. The turn-over in boats, the readily assessable market value, and the established profit margins, which exist in the car market do not, and are never likely to apply to boats. Thus it is that most people when deciding to change their boats do so by private contract or through a broker. We discuss brokers in more detail in chapter 7, but it should be appreciated that when a boat is bought through a broker he is usually acting as the agent of the seller, and is not himself selling the boat. However, some brokers do act as agent for the buyer, especially when he is seeking a particular class or type of vessel and requires specialist help in that regard. There are also some people acting on the fringe of the trade who call themselves 'consultants', whose primary purpose is to act for the purchaser. In these cases the buyer will be obliged to pay agreed fees to his agent, but of course, in a normal sale by a broker the vendor pays the fees. In any event, because the broker or consultant is in business it is possible that the protection under the sale of goods laws may be restored to the buyer in respect of second hand vessels.

If any misrepresentation has been made and forms a part of the contract the position is different, and this principle applies whether the boat is bought directly from the vendor or through a broker. Remember that the contract need not be in writing, although it is preferable that it should be, and any statement by the seller of a vessel which could be held to be a misrepresentation under the terms of the Misrepresentation Act, 1967 would give the buyer the right to rescind the contract, or to seek damages.

Now this is a very important matter for the buyer of second hand boats, because most yachtsmen when selling their beloved craft have a very rosy view of her condition, capabilities and value. It is only necessary to read some of the classified advertisements in the yachting journals to see that objectivity is sometimes missing from the descriptions of craft offered. It was once said that choosing a boat was rather like choosing a wife, with the exception that one actively sought the boat rather than the other way around. Casting that aside, however, it is a sad fact that some degree of emotion plays a part in most purchases of yachts. In the seller you have a man who believes that he is offering the best thing since the ark, and the buyer may be a man who, if the boat has already taken his fancy, lets his anticipation of delights to come blind him to reality. It is out of such circumstances that the stuff of litigation is made.

In order to take advantage of the protection of the Misrepresentation Act, it is necessary to show that the misrepresentation formed a part of the contract, and that the contract has actually been completed, that is, the money has been paid over, and ownership of the vessel has passed to the buyer. If the sale takes place as the result of an advertisement, or through printed details obtained from a broker which contain the misrepresent-ation, then it may be that the misrepresentation was a part of the contract and, subject to the relevant advertisement or sales sheet being capable of proof, the buyer would be able to exercise his rights under the Act. But if the misrepresentation occurs during conversation, as is much more likely, then it would be difficult for the buyer to prove his case unless he had a reliable witness. Verbal statements form a part of a contract if relevant to the deal, but no court is likely to take the word of the buyer against that of the seller in the absence of corroborating evidence. All the same the seller of a yacht should be careful, because there are cases on record where conversations have been accepted by the courts as good evidence.

When buying a second hand yacht by direct negotiation with the owner it is wise to have a written agreement. This is seldom done, especially in regard to unregistered vessels, but in the absence of such a contract the redress of problems is likely to be impossible. The contract, which can be a simple hand written sheet, may take the form recommended in Appendix A. The document should be signed by both parties to the contract in the presence of witnesses, and both should retain a copy.

In the case of a registered vessel there are certain procedures with which both seller and buyer are lawfully bound to comply, under the Merchant Shipping Act, 1894. Whilst this is one of those laws which is not actively enforced, it does exist, and it is as well to follow laid down procedures. Failure to do so could result in serious difficulties if there should ever be a problem of disputed ownership. The Registrar of British Ships in the Port of Registry as shown on the yacht's certificate will advise on forms required and the procedure to be followed. It is not at all complicated but it must be done correctly as the process is controlled by statute. Problems arise when previous changes of ownership have not been registered, and it would be as well for the buyer to obtain a Transcript of Registry from the Registrar of Ships prior to completion of the purchase. This document will show whether there are any charges registered against the vessel (mort-gages and the like) and whether or not the present owner's interest is properly shown. There have been many cases where it has taken several years to sort out registration problems, usually due to previous owners not having registered their interest. In these circumstances it is necessary to obtain Bills of Sale and Declarations of Ownership from previous owners in order to prove continuity through to the present owner. This can be a laborious process and is sometimes almost impossible to achieve.

When buying a second hand yacht through a broker the buyer should remember that although the broker is merely the agent of the seller, it will be necessary to sign a contract in a form supplied by the broker if it is decided to proceed with a purchase. We discuss brokers in more detail in chapter 7, but the advice for sellers contained in that chapter applies equally to the buyer who may be considering whether to do business with a broker. In the author's view there is much to be said for buying a boat through a good broker, and this is especially true for the inexperienced buyer. Not only will the broker steer the buyer clear of hazards, but the form of contract used by him may actually enhance the legal standing of the buyer as we now see.

The law relating to a second hand yacht bought through a broker but from a private seller is that if the buyer does not know that the seller is a private individual or reasonable steps are not taken by the broker to inform him of the fact, then the law of fitness for purpose and merchantable quality does apply. But this is very rarely the case, for even if specific mention is not made of the status of the seller, it is usually clear to the buyer that the broker is acting for a private yachtsman. It is invariably the case that reference is made to the seller by the broker in the presence of, or within the knowledge of, the buyer, and it is likely that the protection of the sale of goods law is not, as a general rule, available to buyers of second hand yachts through brokers.

In cases where a broker is selling a yacht on behalf of a charter company or other commercial user of yachts, then the full protection of the law is available because the seller is acting in the normal course of his business.

The form of contract between a broker and the buyer is obviously very important, and the current form in use by most good brokers is one devised by the Association of Brokers and Yacht Agents with the approval of the Royal Yachting Association. The Yacht Brokers, Designers and Surveyors Association also have a sale and purchase agreement similar in most respects to that of the ABYA. We will discuss the ABYA and the YBDSA in chapter 7, but it is known that these two bodies, with the co-operation of the RYA are currently considering a new form of agreement to be used by all their members. The current form of contract used by brokers who are members of the ABYA and/or the YBDSA is excellent, and no doubt the new one will be better still. It is strongly recommended that buyers of second hand yachts should go to a broker who is a member of one of these two associations and is using the approved form of agreement.

An agreement for the sale of a second hand yacht through a broker should begin by stipulating the agreed price of the vessel, but make it absolutely clear that this sum only becomes due, and the buyer is only finally committed to the contract, when a survey, should the buyer decide to have one, is satisfactorily completed. It is usual for a sum of not more than 10% of the agreed price to be paid to the broker, whereupon he will hold the vessel for the buyer until the survey is complete. The deposit must be returnable should the buyer find reason not to proceed as a result of survey.

It is essential for the contract to stipulate an agreed number of days after which the survey must have been completed. Failure to complete within the stated time by the buyer means that he is committed to the purchase and cannot legally rescind the contract for any reason. The contract should also lay down the number of days after the expiry of the period permitted for survey, by which the buyer must complete. This is important from the seller's point of view for it is not unusual for impecunious buyers to delay completion whilst trying to raise the necessary money. The broker will advise on the services of a surveyor, and the number of days entered into the contract for the survey to be completed is open to negotiation, depending upon the availability of the selected surveyor, and the ability of the chosen yard to lift the vessel out of the water if necessary.

A survey by a professionally qualified and competent surveyor is vital. We discuss the employment of surveyors in chapter 8, but unless the vessel is a dinghy or runabout which can be carefully examined by the buyer who is willing to take a chance on hidden defects, it is most unwise to buy without a survey. In the case of a £10,000 yacht the cost of a survey, including lifting out, making good after the survey and re-launching, is unlikely to exceed £250. Compared with the cost of rectifying hidden faults that is a small sum which should be regarded as a part of the investment. In any case, possession of a recent survey report is useful in matters of re-sale and insurance. However, a surveyor's report should not be regarded as a guarantee that all is well with the vessel. Problems can arise, especially with GRP vessels, which could not be detected by a surveyor, no matter how competent, and the courts have ruled that a survey report does not remove responsibility from the seller, nor detract from the rights of the buyer.

Defects and deficiencies found during the inspection and/or survey are dealt with in an important clause in the contract. The clause reads:-

Within . . . . . . days after completion of such inspection and/or survey, if any material defect or defects in the yacht or its machinery or any material deficiencies in its inventory if any, shall have been found the purchaser may either

(a) give notice to the vendor or brokers of his rejection of the yacht provided that the notice shall specify the material defect or deficiencies or,

(b) give notice to the vendor or brokers specifying the material defects or deficiencies and requiring the vendor forthwith either to make good the same or make a sufficient reduction in the purchase price to enable the purchaser to make good the same.

If the purchaser shall serve notice under sub-clause (a) hereof or if the vendor shall not within 21 days of the serving on him of a notice under sub-clause (b) hereof have agreed to make good without delay the material defect or deficiencies specified by the purchaser in such a notice or if on the service of such a notice the parties are unable to agree within 21 days thereafter upon the amount by which the purchase price is to be reduced this agreement shall be rescinded.

In the event of this agreement being rescinded under any provisions of the above clause the purchaser shall forthwith close up the yacht, make good any damage caused by the survey, and return it to its former position. The vendor shall thereupon return or procure the return of the deposit to the purchaser without deduction and without interest and neither party shall thenceforward have any further claim against the other under this agreement.

The all important word in this clause is *material*. It is not defined in legal terms, and if there were to be litigation based upon this clause the courts would consider what is reasonable, taking into account the type of vessel, its construction, age and value. The advice of the surveyor and the broker would be of assistance to a yachtsman who was unsure of his position here. A relatively minor defect in a near new boat would be regarded as being material, assuming the price agreed reflected market value for the type of boat in good condition. In an older boat minor repairs and maintenance requirements would be unlikely to be considered material. The point is, perhaps, best illustrated by reference to the shaft, since most boats have one. In a near new boat any noticeable wear in the shaft would probably be considered material, and the responsibility of the vendor, whereas in a boat of four or five years of age some wear on the propellor shaft would be accepted as fair wear and tear. In an extreme case, in an older boat where the shaft has worn to a stage where it is necessary to replace it, another situation arises. The purchaser was intending to buy an old boat which by implication will have suffered some wear and tear. The shaft must be replaced, and he will therefore have a new shaft with a considerably longer life than the shaft he might have expected at the outset. In this situation the chances are that the vendor will pay a percentage of the cost and the purchaser the rest, as there is clearly an element of improvement involved.

It must be pointed out that if the vendor or the purchaser adopts an unreasonable attitude in dealing with problems of this kind the clause is of little value. But the clause is a brave attempt by the ABYA and the YBDSA to resolve what can be a difficult problem. The advice and wise counsel of a good broker can often help to iron out such problems.

The agreement form contains sections on the acceptance of the yacht. Once all the stages relative to the survey and the rectification of faults or deficiencies, if any, have been completed, or, if there has been no survey, a period of 14 days has passed since the signing of the agreement, then the buyer is legally responsible for the yacht and the remainder of the money outstanding on it. As soon as the buyer offers the outstanding sums due he must be given a properly executed Bill of Sale together with the certificate of registration and any other relevant documents. It is the buyer's responsibility to have the registration transferred to his name.

The clause in the agreement relating to acceptance contains one sentence which is common in broker's agreements, and is probably illegal. It states:-

The purchaser shall thereupon take possession of the yacht, which shall be taken with all errors and faults of description without any allowance or abatement whatsoever.

Since the provisions of the Misrepresentation Act, 1967 and the Unfair Contract Terms Act, 1977 do apply to agreements of this type, this clause cannot have any effect. It is also a criminal offence to insert any statement in a contract which may mislead a buyer as to his rights. The ABYA Sale and Purchase Agreement is under review at the time of writing, and it is likely that this clause will be omitted from future agreement forms. The new form will confirm the statutory rights of the purchaser. However, it is possible that brokers who are not members of the ABYA or the YBDSA (see chapter 7) will continue to use agreement forms which do contain such a clause. Yachtsmen should not be misled by it.

In the event of a purchaser failing to pay over the balance of the purchase price after the agreed period has elapsed, the seller, after giving fourteen days notice of his intention to the buyer, may sell the yacht elsewhere. Furthermore, the original purchaser would lose his deposit and would be liable for any losses sustained by the seller through having to re-advertise or being obliged to accept a lower price than that originally agreed. These are harsh penalties indeed against a buyer but they are necessary to ensure that business is done smoothly. It should always be borne in mind however, that should the purchaser be delayed through no fault of his own, such as illness, the courts would take a lenient view and would not support a seller who insisted on the precise letter of the agreement. In this, as in all matters, the courts expect the parties to a contract to behave reasonably.

Finally, the contract contains provision for the resolution of disputes by arbitration in the same way as that discussed in chapter 5.

We have been discussing a good contract used by a good broker, but it is sad to reflect that such business-like agreements are not always used. Some very difficult problems can arise if a badly worded agreement is used, and such problems are worse still if no written agreement exists. It is often tempting to buy a yacht privately in the belief that it will be cheaper because the seller will not be incurring brokerage fees. There is little evidence that yachts sold privately are in fact any cheaper than those sold by good brokers, and by dealing with a good broker the buyer gains potentially a great deal of protection. On the other hand there are a few rogues in the brokerage business, as in any other walk of life, and the advice given to sellers in the next chapter about the selection of a good broker applies equally to the buyer.

If a yacht or equipment has been stolen and is bought in good faith by a yachtsman, he will lose it if it is traced by the police or the legal owner. It is only in the case of what is called a 'market overt' (open market) that a buyer of stolen goods is deemed to be the legal owner. Yachts and equipment are not, generally speaking, sold in markets overt. The number of boats and equipment being stolen these days and finding their way back on to the second hand market poses a risk to any buyer dealing directly with a private seller. A good broker, with his knowledge of the market and his considerable 'grape vine' in the trade might spot such dangers whereas the private buyer on his own would not.

If a yacht or equipment is sold whilst still subject to a credit agreement in the name of the previous owner, the buyer is deemed to be the legal owner, and it cannot be recovered by the creditor. The debtor, whoever he might be, is liable at civil and criminal law for his actions. But the buyer could be put to a great deal of trouble and be subjected to some tedious investigations. It is as well to enquire of the seller about possible debts still outstanding on the goods he is offering. If the vessel is registered there is value in obtaining a transcript of the Registry before completion in order to establish that no charges are registered and that the vendor is in fact the registered owner.

The sale of second hand boats built by amateurs from kits is creating problems for second hand buyers. The rapid growth of the home completion market means that an increasing number of boats are finding their way from this source on to the second hand market. Many of them are finished just as well as the professionally built models, but others are not. In any event home built boats do not command the same prices on the second hand market, and there is therefore a built-in incentive for the seller to conceal the fact, if possible, that the craft is home built.

It is entirely possible that the advertising of a vessel under its class name without any mention of the fact that it is home built could not only be deemed to be a breach of the Trade Descriptions Act, 1968 but could also be a misrepresentation under the Misrepresentation Act, 1967. This would depend upon whether the vendor could be held to have deliberately attempted to conceal the fact that the boat was built by an amateur, or, given ample opportunity to tell the buyer, had neglected to do so.

This matter does not yet appear to have been tested in the courts, but problems are now arising with such frequency that such an event cannot be long delayed.

7 Selling A Yacht

There comes a time in the life of every yachtsman when he decides to change his boat, usually for something bigger. The question then arises of how to dispose of his existing craft, at the best price, and at a time convenient for the purchase of the new vessel. The best course of action is often dictated by the time of the year, the availability of cash, prevailing rates of interest, and the type of craft for disposal. In essence, however, the first question to be answered is whether to attempt to sell the yacht privately by advertisement in the yachting press, or whether to employ a broker.

If the decision is to sell privately the first question to be asked is what the price should be. This is difficult, because the period of rapid inflation in the value of boats which took place in 1975 and 1976 has distorted market values. Furthermore, rapid technological developments in the marine industry and the enormous variety of boats available have resulted in a very fluid situation in second hand boat markets. A glance at the classified advertisements for boats shows some remarkable variations in asking prices for similar craft which tends to confirm that most private sellers have considerable difficulty in assessing the value of their boats. The truth is that the value of any object is the price a buyer is willing to pay, and all the private seller can do is study the market, check on asking prices for similar craft, adjust up or down for equipment, age and condition, and then set a realistic target price. The problem is easy enough to solve if one is selling a very popular craft such as a Westerly Centaur. There are so many on the market at any one time that it is easy to assess the market value. It is much more difficult to set a realistic price for a one-off design.

Many yachtsmen make the mistake of asking greatly inflated prices, thinking that they can always reduce if necessary. Experience suggests that to ask too much at the outset creates a resistance to the sale, which later reductions cannot overcome. Indeed, dramatic price reductions sometimes suggest either a fault in the vessel or that the seller is avaricious – neither of which is necessarily the case. There are available some guides to the value of class boats but in the experience of the author they are unreliable, and the range of prices they are obliged to quote for a particular class is so wide as to render them meaningless.

The next step is to draft an advertisement. It should be appreciated at the outset that the criminal sanctions in the Trade Descriptions Act 1968 do not apply to private sellers, and the remedies at civil law in relation to merchantable quality and fitness for purpose are not available to buyers from private sellers. Thus there is nothing in law to restrict what may be said in a private advertisement other than the provisions of the Misrepresentation Act, 1967. Even here it would be necessary for the buyer to prove that the misrepresentation was of a substantial nature, formed a part of the contract, and involved him in some significant loss. Thus it is safe to describe the vessel offered in the most favourable terms without fear of the consequences, but no honourable yachtsman would deliberately falsify details of his craft. It is particularly important that the condition and previous history of the yacht, if mentioned in the advertisement, should be truthfully stated, for any misleading impressions given could lead to serious consequences for the seller. This is particularly the case these days when interest in yachting is expanding rapidly and more first time buyers are entering the market. The courts are likely to take a serious view of a seller who deliberately misleads a gullible first time buyer.

It is wise to have a duplicated sheet of details of the vessel together with a photograph, available for enquirers. A note of the date of building, class, dimensions, accommodation, and history, together with a full inventory, creates a favourable impression. Again it should be realised that truthfulness is important because the sheet could be held to be evidence in an action for misrepresentation, and it is particularly important that only those items for sale should be included in the inventory. There have been endless disputes over missing items which the seller decided at the last moment to keep.

The next stage is the inspection of the craft by potential buyers. If the owner is able to show people over his yacht himself, well and good, because he will be able to demonstrate her and ensure that she is properly described. But if he relies on a friend or a yard to demonstrate her he has no control over what they may say or do, although in law he would be liable for any misrepresentations made by them. They would be deemed to be acting as his agent. There is also the need to ensure that the boat is properly closed up after each inspection. It is a sad fact that there is a growing army of 'boat viewers' – people who have no serious intention of buying, but who seem to obtain some amusement from looking over craft for sale, and trying them out at sea. They care little for the property of other people and unless they are accompanied and carefully supervised it may be that damage or loss will occur. The private seller of a boat who cannot be personally present when potential buyers are viewing is vulnerable. He should, at the very least, ensure that his insurance cover is good for such risks.

A potential new owner will wish to have a survey done once a price is agreed. We have seen in chapter 6 the sort of agreement used for the sale of a second hand yacht by a good broker which includes a clause to protect the owner of a vessel against damage done by surveyors, the cost of making that damage good, hauling out, and re-launching etc. There is also the vital question of time limits on the carrying out of the survey and the completion of the contract thereafter. In most private sales of yachts few documents are used beyond a transfer of ownership and a receipt. It would be wise to use a simple form of contract as recommended in appendix A.

Once the survey is complete, and the final price agreed, it is important **to ensure that the cheque or other form of payment is good.** To part with the vessel before the cash is guaranteed is unwise, even if the registration has not been changed. In law the ownership of the vessel would not be considered to have passed to the buyer until the money has been paid over, the registration has been changed, and the vessel has been physically handed over to the buyer. But these rules can be changed by agreement, and if the seller has handed over the yacht before all the money has been received, it would be possible for the buyer to argue, in the absence of documentary evidence to the contrary, that the seller agreed that he should take the yacht and full payments could be deferred.

If possession of the yacht is surrendered to the buyer before the cash is received it may be that the owner's insurance will automatically lapse. Damage occurring to the vessel whilst in the hands of the new owner may not, in such circumstances, be claimed against the seller's insurance policy.

The golden rule is not to part with property until the cash is in hand, no matter how impressive the status of the buyer appears to be. There are a considerable number of pitfalls into which a yachtsman may fall if he decides to sell his vessel privately. There are an increasing number of unscrupulous buyers adept at creating contractual traps for the unwary. Unless the private seller is confident of his ability to forsee these pitfalls and avoid them it may be wise to employ a good broker.

If it is decided to sell the craft through a broker it is as well to know something about the way brokers work and who they are. The first thing which strikes one about brokers is that there are a great many of them. There are sixteen listed in the yellow pages of the Portsmouth telephone directory alone, and they represent a substantial industry in their own right. Many of them have been in business, or have been associated with yachting all their lives and are very knowledgeable, but at the moment there is no qualification required for anyone to act as a yacht broker. A man could be a left hand Cortina ash tray fitter one day and a yacht broker the next. His customers would be none the wiser.

On a personal basis many brokers belong to **the Yacht Brokers, Designers and Surveyors Association (YBDSA)** which dates back to 1912. The association numbers amongst its members many of the leading brokers in the United Kingdom and abroad. The YBDSA has a well deserved reputation for being outward looking and cooperative with the yachting public and writers, which is far from the case with some other professional and trade associations. The association will not admit a broker to full membership unless he has had continuous business experience for not less than three years and is of good reputation. Its rules prescribe admirable standards of conduct for all members, with a final sanction of expulsion from the association for serious breaches of professional ethics.

The Association of Brokers and Yacht Agents (ABYA) consists not of individual brokers, but of brokerage firms. Many brokers whose firms belong to the ABYA are also members of YBDSA, and the aims and objectives of the two associations are very similar. The membership list of ABYA includes most of the major firms in the business, and a firm cannot be admitted to membership unless it has traded for a minimum of three years. The ABYA, which has been in existence for 22 years, is in essence a part of the SBBNF (see chapter 3) since all firms which belong to ABYA are also members of SBBNF. Together they form what is known as the "British Boating Industry" and in 1979 membership list of ABYA contains the names of the leading 111 brokerage firms in the United Kingdom. The number of individual brokers associated with companies which are in membership of ABYA is estimated to be in excess of 300.

The ABYA is currently endeavouring to devise a diploma course for yacht brokers which may, in the long term, result in a qualification which will be recognised as standard throughout the industry. But more important from the point of view of the yachtsman, is the British Boating

Industry Code of Practice for the sale of used boats which is now formally accepted by the SBBNF, ABYA and YBDSA. Although the code is essentially a trade agreement it does impose stringent conditions on brokers as to how they should conduct their business and indirectly enhances the position of yachtsmen who do business with member brokers. More important still the ABYA and YBDSA are working jointly on a new Code of Practice which will relate entirely to dealings with the public, and will be published. If the new Code of Practice is approved by the Director General of Fair Trading under his powers under the Fair Trading Act, 1973, the code will be a major step forward in consumer protection for the yachtsman.

But what services can a broker provide for the yachtsman? This is perhaps best answered by quoting from the YBDSA's own leaflet:-

The broker brings together buyers and sellers of yachts of all types and values thereby obtaining details of craft for sale in all parts of the world, and is therefore able to offer a suitable selection to prospective buyers. He acts as an intermediary between buyer and seller during negotiations and completes all the formalities for the transfer of title when negotiations are completed. The broker can advise the seller from varied experience the likely price of the vessel and naturally endeavour to obtain the highest figure which in turn earns the appropriate commission. The advice will, however, recognise that an over priced yacht that does not sell is of no use to its vendor or the broker. The broker acts for the seller in the course of the sale and ensures that the title is not transferred until the total purchase price is in his hands. When appointed SOLE AGENT the broker will in turn appoint sub-agents, providing them with all assistance and accordingly widening the market.

The broker offers the buyer the widest selection and helps to simplify his search to a few likely vessels and arranges the inspections. When the buyer makes his choice the broker undertakes the negotiations, can make arrangements for survey and provide a short list of reputable yacht surveyors, leaving the choice to the buyer. The broker can also prepare the Sale Agreement utilising a standard form of contract prepared by the YBDSA obviating legal fees. Following survey he can assist in any further negotiations and finally prepares the Bill of Sale and hands over all the documents in exchange for the purchase money, thus giving clear title to the new owner. Brokers also assist with registration problems such as changes of name, and in some cases undertake valuations.

The broker's income derives from sale commission fees paid by the vendors and the stated services are covered by those fees, there being no other charge to owners or buyers except where a definite service is performed unrelated to a sale or charter.

It should be noted that the form of contract used by YBDSA and ABYA is virtually the same and the scale of commission charged by members of both bodies is the same.

It is clear that high professional standards are demanded of members by both the ABYA and YBDSA, but when deciding to do business with a broker the yachtsman should consider his choice carefully. The fact is that a broker's commission due on the sale of a yacht is a significant sum, say £400 on a £5,000 vessel, but that is money well spent if all the services offered are in fact discharged efficiently. Whilst there is no guarantee that a broker in membership of ABYA and/or YBDSA will be efficient, there is obviously a better chance that he will be more professionally competent than a broker who does not enjoy such membership. The member broker has voluntarily submitted himself to the rules of the associations and has promised to abide by the code of practice. It is worth bearing the following factors in mind when selecting a broker:-

1. Personal recommendations from friends and acquaintances including fellow club members are always a valuable guide. The yachting fraternity has an excellent 'grape vine' and although tall stories tend to be told over the club bar, much good information can be obtained there too.

2. Look at the quantity, style and quality of a broker's advertising. A great deal can be learnt from advertisements in the major yachting journals. Be suspicious of the broker who uses superlatives to excess.

3. The presentation and content of particulars of yachts for sale can tell a good deal about a broker.

4. Good brokers have a detailed questionnaire form for boats. How comprehensive is it? Would it give all the information you would seek if you were a buyer, and does it remind you of your responsibilities under the Misrepresentation Act?

5. Is the broker in membership of ABYA and/or YBDSA?

6. What impression is created at the broker's offices, and where are they located? Does he make you feel that he has a genuine interest in selling the vessel; does his office give an impression of efficiency; and is it located near to a major yachting centre?

Having decided upon a broker it is important to realise that the seller is entering into a contract of service with him. Like any other contract it is all the better for being clearly defined and written down. A good broker will ask the vendor to complete a detailed questionnaire setting out the price to be asked, full information about the vessel, her equipment, history and condition, and where she may be inspected. This questionnaire is the basis of the contract, and it should be accompanied by a covering letter, an example of which is given in appendix B. Beware of the broker who supplies no questionnaire and merely writes a letter setting out the scale of commission to be charged on the introduction of a buyer. This is not good enough, for there are a host of things which could go wrong in the absence of a clearly defined agreement.

Some brokers prefer to be appointed as the SOLE AGENT. Whether this is beneficial to the vendor depends entirely upon the circumstances, for the meaning of the term varies between brokers. To appoint a small broker who is not a member of ABYA or YBDSA as a sole agent is probably unwise for he will not have the contacts with the bulk of the brokerage business to circulate information about the vessel. The term 'sole agent' is now largely outmoded, for the ABYA and YBDSA are trying to establish the principle of 'Central Listing'. This means that in return for exclusive instructions to offer the yacht for sale, the broker promises to circulate comprehensive illustrated particulars of the vessel to selected brokers, and offers them half the commission due if they should find a buyer. This is done in addition to the normal advertising and promotion of the sale by the centrally listed broker. Where a central listing agreement is given in writing and forms a part of the contract with the broker there are obvious advantages to the vendor in such an agreement.

If it is desired to sell privately in addition to instructing a broker, care should be taken to ensure that this is clearly understood by the broker. Generally speaking brokers are not happy about such arrangements because unscrupulous vendors may attempt to evade paying commission. It is often open to doubt whether an enquirer has responded to a broker's advertisement or one published by the vendor privately. Few brokers would agree to a central listing if the vendor were also going to try to sell privately. If a vendor has genuinely found his own buyer, but would prefer a broker to handle the formalities of the sale, it is often possible for this to be arranged for about half the normal rates of commission.

Brokers should be given clear instructions about the arrangements for viewing the craft for sale. There is an unfortunate practice amongst a few brokers, of simply handing out keys of yachts to enquirers and letting them look over boats unaccompanied. As a result damage may be done for which the broker would not be liable unless specific instructions had been given to the contrary. Some brokers may claim that there is general overall supervision by dockmasters and marina staff, and that a representative is not needed on board every time a boat is viewed. However, in the experience of the author it is wise to give specific instructions on this point. An appropriate wording is recommended in appendix B.

When the decision to buy has been taken a good broker will

recommend a survey and will provide a short list of recommended surveyors. The choice is, of course, a matter for the buyer, but it may be wise for the seller to enquire of the broker which surveyors he intends to recommend. The rules of the British Boating Industry, and therefore the ABYA and the YBDSA, specifically forbid a broker from having special arrangements to pass work to favoured surveyors, and if a broker is known to do this sort of thing, then the vendor should ponder the dangers of instructing him to sell.

The rate of commission sought by the broker should be that recommended in the British Boating Industry Code of Practice, and the broker should be willing to confirm that this is so. Beware of the broker who will give no such assurance, for there are non-member brokers who are known to charge above the recommended rate. Beware also of the broker who seeks to justify higher than usual commission on the grounds that he is giving a superior service. The broker who immediately gives an assurance that he has a client waiting for the very boat offered, and can arrange a quick sale for a high rate of commission is likely to be a rogue.

The publicity material put out by brokers about vessels for sale can, if false or misleading, constitute an offence against the Trade Descriptions Act, 1968. The Act does not, however, apply to private citizens and so it is conceivable that a broker could face a criminal prosecution for simply repeating information given to him about a craft. This is not as harsh as it sounds, because the Trade Descriptions Act, in common with other consumer protection legislation, expects people in business to know their business. They should check that what they are saying is accurate. In law this is called 'exercising due diligence to avoid the commission of an offence'. A good broker would not be so foolish as to publish an advertisement which contained false statements, but a rogue broker, to whom the truth would have no meaning, might be willing to chance his arm. If he was caught he would probably plead in defence that he had been misled by the owner, who could find himself in the embarassing position of having to give evidence in a criminal trial about the sale of his own boat. This is another reason for doing business only with good brokers.

If a broker claims to be a member of ABYA, YBDSA, or any other professional body, whilst not holding such membership he commits an offence against the Trade Desriptions Act. The matter should be reported to the Trading Standards or Consumer Protection Department of the local authority.

Finally, a yacht broker can be sued for negligence, and he cannot rely upon any disclaimers which seek to limit his liability unless such limitation is reasonable within the meaning of the Unfair Contract Terms Act, 1977. There have never, within the knowledge of the author, been any cases where yachtsmen have been obliged to sue a broker for negligence, but it is conceivable that a negligent broker could be held liable for damages if he could be shown to have lost an advantageous sale for his client.

8 Employing A Surveyor

Surveyors, like brokers, need no special qualifications or experience to start up in business. The consequences of this can be that a bad surveyor is likely to be much more dangerous than a bad broker, for he is dealing with very costly matters and, on occasions, it may be a question of life or death. If that sounds over-dramatic, it is only a question of considering the possibility of a newcomer to yachting buying his first vessel on the recommendation of an inefficient surveyor and setting off to sea in her. She may be thoroughly unseaworthy, but the owner has taken all the precautions that could be expected of him.

Some surveyors are chartered engineers and/or members or fellows of the Royal Institute of Naval Architects. Many of them are also members of the Yacht Brokers, Designers and Surveyors Association. Although letters after a name do not make a man, and the absence of letters does not necessarily mean a lack of expertise, it is obviously, on balance, safer to go for the qualified man.

What does a surveyor claim to be able to do? The current literature of the YBDSA says of surveyors:-

The primary function of the surveyor is to ascertain the condition of the vessel, namely that of its structure, rig, machinery, and gear. Within the limitations of time and the circumstances of the survey, he will ascertain the facts as to wear and tear, disease of timber, corrosion of metals, and crazing of GRP (glass fibre). He will also know whether the structure is correctly executed and a survey can thus apply to a new vessel. 'Structure' is another all embracing description and applies not merely to the main members such as planking, plating or mouldings, but to the bolt or nail or rivet fastenings, to rigging, chain plates or shaft brackets.

There are also installations such as steering gears, even if only a humble wood rudder and tiller, in fact structure of every part of the vessel. The surveyor basically has a full knowledge of yacht and boat construction in all types of materials and additionally becomes part biologist, botanist, chemist, metallurgist, engineer, and possibly navigator. He does not merely 'find out if the wood is rotten' or 'fail' or 'pass' a yacht, but his report is an overall assessment of her condition from which her potential can be deduced. The most common form of survey is required when a yacht is purchased and the cost of a good survey is literally the price of guaranteeing the investment of the purchase price. The buyer always instructs and pays the surveyor whose report is for the buyer's exclusive information. Under the YBDSA rules, surveyors are not allowed to accept any share of sale commission or payments from other parties concerned unless in special circumstances they may have the approval of the buyer. The rules also prohibit the practice of exclusion of liability for negligence when instructed to carry out a survey; such exclusions not applying to ordinary inspections.

Surveyors can also carry out surveys of damage following accidents for insurance purposes. Specifying and supervising work for repairs and modifications, diagnosing possible defects and inspecting and valuing vessels prior to purchase are also operations undertaken by surveyors.

Impressive stuff indeed; perhaps a little fanciful; but it does illustrate the attempt by the YBDSA to maintain high standards of professional competence amongst its members. Of those members there are 66 surveyors listed in the current membership roll of the YBDSA in the United Kingdom and abroad. It therefore follows that there are many people claiming to be surveyors who are not members of YBDSA nor, apparently of any other professional body.

A full survey of a yacht is not cheap, and on a £10,000 vessel can cost upwards of £250 if the cost of hauling out, making good and re-launching are included. It is not surprising therefore, that many buyers seek reasons for not employing a surveyor, reasons such as 'she is only five years old, and a good yacht does not need a survey until her seventh or eighth year', or 'I have seen the previous owner's survey report which is only three years old', or 'the owner himself is a marine engineer and he assures me that all is well', and so on. It is always tempting to make excuses for not spending money and these remarks are typical of those made every year by hundreds of buyers of second hand yachts. They are very foolish. The cost of a survey amounts to a very small percentage of the total cost of buying a yacht, and would be a mere fraction of rectifying a major fault. Although a survey can never be a guarantee that there are no faults, a good surveyor can so minimise the risk inherent in the purchase of every yacht that his fees become well worth while.

The reasons given for not having a survey are nearly all fallacious.

The fact that a yacht is of relatively recent construction is not a reason for avoiding a survey. Quite the contrary. For one thing it takes no account of any damage she may have sustained under the command of her first owner – damage which may have been badly repaired, and it does not allow for the fact that the hull may have had inherent faults during construction which only reveal themselves after a season or two of use. This is particularly the case with GRP hulls, as owners with problems of osmosis will confirm. For the same reasons an old survey report, which may have some value nevertheless cannot take into account recent damage. The suggestion that a survey is unnecessary because the owner himself is knowledgeable is, of course, too absurd to be taken seriously. In fact any owner who suggested that a survey on his yacht was unnecessary because of his own expertise would be immediately suspect. Beware also of the knowledgeable 'yachting friend' who so exudes nautical know-how that the gullible buyer is tempted to use his services rather than employ a proper surveyor. He is likely to be the most useless of them all.

The selection of a surveyor is of crucial importance in the absence of any indicators as to competence other than membership of a professional association. It is unwise to employ a surveyor recommended by the seller or his broker; their recommendation may be perfectly sincere and genuine, but it is bad practice all the same. The best recommendation is personal experience of surveyors, and if the buyer has none then the local yacht club may be able to help. Once it has been decided to employ a particular surveyor to do the job it would be reasonable to enquire if he has any previous experience of the class of yacht concerned and the form of construction. There are still some older surveyors who are not very knowledgeable about GRP, and likewise some younger ones have not gained much experience with timber and steel. It would also be wise to ask about technical recources. Is the surveyor, for example, going to use X-ray equipment for the keel bolts, can he detect the source and recommend the cure for electrolysis, and has he the necessary guages to do a thorough check on the engine? No professional surveyor would object to genuine questions of this type.

It is then necessary to decide how far the surveyor should go in his work. The more he does the more he will charge, the less he does the more useless it becomes to employ him at all. The question to be decided is how much of a risk the buyer is willing to take? It may be that a new engine has recently been fitted which is still subject to a manufacturer's guarantee. In that case it would be reasonable to ask the surveyor to confine his examination to the installation of the engine thus saving in costs. It may be that the buyer intends to replace the standing and running rigging, and perhaps the sails too. In that case there is no point in asking the surveyor to examine them. But it is very unwise to make any savings on the hull, skin fittings, and spars.

In appointing a surveyor the yachtsman is entering into a contract of service with him and the surveyor is liable for any negligence he may commit in his discharge of that contract. However, he cannot be accused of negligence if his client's instructions are not made clear to him. The best course of action is to talk to him about the vessel and ask his advice about the principal points to be checked. He is in business, and he is unlikely to suggest that he does less than is necessary. So it is safe to assume, that if he is a competent surveyor, then his advice will amount to the maximum that needs to be done to give reasonable assurance that the craft is sound. Having decided what items, if any, are to be exluded from the survey it is wise to write a letter to the surveyor asking him to carry out the work and giving him full details of the survey to be done.

If the surveyor accepts the letter then there is an enforceable contract. If he thinks the letter is unclear or unreasonable then it is for him to seek clarification or amendment. Remember that by virtue of the Unfair Contract Terms Act, 1977 the surveyor cannot limit his liability for negligence resulting in death or injury at all, and that resulting in loss or damage only to the extent which is reasonable.

It is sometimes asked if it is a good thing to have a survey done on a new yacht. On the whole the answer must be in the affirmative. Of course if the yacht is a very small and relatively cheap one then it would not be economic to do so. Furthermore if the yacht has been bought from one of the very large manufacturers of class vessels in the United Kingdom who offer a quite superb after sales service it is probably unnecessary. But in all other cases it would be wise to have a yacht finally surveyed before final acceptance. A good surveyor can detect faults in manufacture which the owner could never find and the acceptance of the yacht can be deferred until they are rectified. By the very nature of men it is always easier to get things done before the vessel is accepted than after.

It is especially valuable to have a survey done on new yachts imported into the United Kingdom. Although the contractual rights of the buyer lie against the importer, assuming it is he who accepted the contract of sale, there are inevitably problems about structural defects in foreign yachts. A foreign builder is not likely to put skilled workers on an aircraft to come to Britain, nor to employ UK based people to rectify faults in one of his boats unless he is obliged to do so. Rejection of the vessel before acceptance is likely to provide the incentive he needs.

The use of a surveyor to assess accident damage and to ensure that it is properly corrected is one of the most valuable services surveyors provide to yachtsmen. The full extent of collision damage is very difficult to assess and very easy to cover up by inadequate repairs.

9 Buying On Credit

No doubt someone will eventually give a name to the perpetual desire of yachtsmen for a bigger and better yacht. It afflicts all of us from time to time, and when the decision to buy is made the question of raising the money arises. If the buyer is lucky enough to pay cash for his new vessel well enough, although he would be well advised to consider the wisdom of cashing in investments to buy an appreciating asset like a boat. Although there are no reliable figures to show how many people do buy their boats on credit, the volume of sales, and the bewildering variety of sources of credit offered do suggest that credit buying is a major factor in the growth of sailing as a hobby, and of the marine industry in the British economy. Although buying on credit is not as attractive as it once was when income tax allowances were available on marine mortgages, there are still positive advantages providing the source of credit is carefully chosen.

The main forms of credit for boat buying are:-

Personal Loan or Overdraft from one's own bank is, depending upon individual circumstances, still the most flexible and often the cheapest way of raising money. Banks are now much more willing to lend substantial sums to credit worthy private customers than they were a few years ago, and in any case this form of credit is usually charged at about 3% above Bank Rate; it is therefore a good deal cheaper than most other forms of credit.

Hire Purchase is suitable only for relatively small sums and thus for the purchase of dinghies and runabouts etc. It involves a fixed percentage deposit, depending upon the credit controls in force at the time, and interest which is usually levied on the whole amount for the currency of the loan. Although the flat rate of interest quoted may appear to be reasonable the true rate is likely to be very high, and hire purchase is almost inevitably the most expensive way of raising money for boat purchase.

A Personal Loan from a finance company can be more flexible, and may provide a larger loan than could be raised on hire purchase, but it is likely to cost more than a similar loan from a High Street bank.

A Marine Mortgage is much the same as a mortgage on a house, except that the interest rate is usually much higher, and no income tax is allowed in respect of any of the interest paid. Nevertheless, in the absence of funds from a private bank it is, perhaps, the best way to raise money for larger vessels. As a rule marine mortgage companies are not interested in vessels costing less than £2,000 and are most ready to do business on those costing in excess of £10,000. Unlike hire purchase and some personal loans, the interest on marine mortgages is charged on the decreasing capital debt outstanding, and arrangements for early redemption of the debt are possible.

Loans on Life and Endowment Policies are sometimes possible where a policy has been in being for a sufficiently long time to qualify for loan value. The rates of interest and the willingness of the insurance companies to lend money for a boat vary enormously, but in the absence of other sources of finance enquiries may be worth while.

Second Mortgages on Houses are sometimes used by enthusiastic yachtsmen to acquire the boat of their hearts' desire. It is unlikely that a reputable building society would be willing to finance a boat even where the loan would be secured against a house with little or no outstanding mortgage, and this means that it is necessary to seek a second mortgage from one of the many companies specialising in this sort of finance. Although some second mortgage companies do maintain good standards of business integrity, others do not, and it is necessary to be very careful when seeking funds from such sources. Interest rates are usually higher than normal building society rates, there are sometimes commissioning and other charges, and income tax is not allowed against interest even where the loan is secured against a house. It is sometimes suggested that funds can be raised ostensibly for an extension or improvement to a house, and then used for the purchase of a boat. It may be possible to do this, but it would be regarded as deception by the Inland Revenue quite apart from other ethical considerations.

Loans may be put into two classes from the point of view of the law, namely those above and those below £5,000. Loans up to that figure are controlled by the provisions of the Consumer Credit Act, 1974, and those above, for all practical purposes are not. The distinction is an important one, for this massive and daunting piece of legislation provides some very valuable safeguards for the debtor, and a much higher degree of 'caveat emptor' (let the buyer beware) is necessary for loans above £5,000. The thinking behind this distinction is that sums up to £5,000 are normally used to buy consumer goods from shops, and those above for more durable capital assets such as a seagoing yacht. It is assumed by the law that any borrower seeking credit for large sums could be expected to take precautions to protect himself, including the possibility of professional advice from his bank manager or accountant. The figure of £5,000 represents the size of the debt, and not the cost of the goods bought with the money borrowed. Thus a loan of £5,000 on a yacht costing, say £7,500 would be caught by the Act, but a loan of £5,500 on a yacht costing £6,500 would not. Credit in excess of the maximum sum of £5,000 is not absolutely free from control. It is subject to the little known Bills of Sale Acts, 1878 to 1882. A Bill of Sale, as we have seen earlier, is a document which transfers property from one person to another. The transfer may be absolute, or where there is a financial interest in the vessel by another person the Bill of Sale makes record of that interest. These Acts also attempt to prevent the use of oppressive terms against a debtor, but they are seldom invoked, perhaps because the high standards of professional advice available to borrowers in the United Kingdom tend to prevent trouble arising.

The maximum figure of £5,000 under the Consumer Credit Act, 1974 seemed high enough when the Act was being drafted in 1973, but since the value of money has halved since that date it now seems rather less suitable. It is likely that the figure will be substantially raised within the next few years, and it would be wise for any yachtsman seeking finance for a yacht to determine what the current maximum figure is before concluding a deal. The degree of protection available to him, and consequently the care to be taken in negotiating the finance, depends upon it.

Credit agreements of less than £10 are exempted from the Act and 'small agreements' of between £10 and £30 are covered in regard to default and termination, but are exempted from the more detailed controls relating to withdrawal and cancellation.

The main controls in the Act operate under a system of licencing which is under the supervision of the Director General of Fair Trading. All credit traders are required to hold a valid licence from the Director General and if they indulge in credit trading without such a licence they commit criminal offences and civil wrongs. It is not merely the granters of credit such as the big finance houses and trading companies who are caught by the licensing system. Also covered are people who provide goods for hire, such as life raft leasing companies; credit brokers, such as a yacht broker who arranges finance for his customers; debt adjusters and counsellors, such as brokers or chandlers who arrange the settlement of existing debts to facilitate further transactions; debt collectors, such as agents of finance houses who attempt to collect outstanding debts from impecunious or irresponsible yachtsmen; and credit reference agencies, such as those who keep records of the credit worthiness of yachtsmen for finance houses.

The canvassing of credit, that is the calling univited upon potential customers by salesmen offering credit facilities, is illegal.

Unlicenced credit traders run the risk of prosecution by the Trading Standards department of County Councils but they would also find, in the event of their clients' breaking an agreement that the agreement is unenforceable. This means that an unlicenced seller of boats or equipment on credit would be unable to recover his money in the courts if his customers simply refused to keep up with their payments.

The Act contains new and valuable provisions in regard to liability for misrepresentation and breach of contract. Where goods are bought on credit and the credit relates specifically to the goods themselves, i.e. the goods are not bought through Access or Barclaycard or some other form of revolving credit, – then the seller and the creditor **are jointly liable in respect of such matters as merchantable quality, fitness for purpose, and so on.** This means that if a boat is bought by way of credit from a bank or finance house, and the seller goes out of business or will not meet his liabilities the creditor would still be liable. Thus there are definite advantages to buying on credit where the viability of the seller is suspect. The effects of this interesting new provision are likely to be that finance companies and banks will be much more careful about financing transactions through sellers whose business methods or financial standing are suspect.

The form of credit agreements and the documents to be used in respect of agreements will depend upon regulations to be made by the Secretary of State. At the time of writing such regulations are still awaited, but the purpose of them will be to give substance to the 'truth in lending' gospel of the Act. By this we mean that the creditor and debtor will know exactly where they stand. Such matters as the early redemption of debts, the appropriate 'cooling off' period during which a borrower may withdraw from an envisaged contract for credit, and so on, will all be clearly set out in the agreement documents and enforceable by the courts.

Credit reference agencies, that is those organisations which compile information about the credit worthiness of customers, have always had a rather tarnished image. The suspicion of sharp practices and gestapo like methods of enquiry is widely held, and few people like the idea of being the subject of a secret dossier to which they have no access. The Act puts this to rights, by giving a statutory right to every debtor or hirer to have information about his credit standing released to him. Requests for information from a credit reference agency must be put into writing, must give sufficient information about the transaction for it to be traced, and must be accompanied by a fee of 25p.

The provisions of the Consumer Credit Act are extremely complex and it is impossible to do full justice to them in one chapter of a book like this one. Any yachtsman who wishes to have further information about his rights and obligations under the Act would be well advised to contact the Trading Standards or Consumer Protection Department of his County Council in England and Wales or his Regional Council in Scotland. In London the appropriate authority is the London Borough. Most authorities employ a specialist in consumer credit matters and can give advice together with a number of explanatory leaflets produced by the Office of Fair Trading. The following steps should be taken by any yachtsman intending to borrow for the purchase of his boat or equipment:-

1. Establish whether the amount to be borrowed falls within the control of the Consumer Credit Act.

2. Check all sources of credit paying particular attention to the true rate of interest, and whether there are any 'service' or 'redemption' charges.

3. Determine whether the agreement gives a right to early redemption of the loan, and what penalties, if any, lie for such redemption.

4. If the loan is by way of hire purchase check that the agreement documents specify the position in regard to seizure of the goods by the creditor in the event of arrears of payments.

5. If the loan is by overdraft or personal loan check whether the creditor is entitled to call in the loan before the expiry of the agreed period.

6. Credit traders are required by law to give details of any credit reference agencies consulted. If they do not offer the information, ask for it, and consider the desirability of asking the agency for details of the file.

7. Do not be enticed by offers of credit from the builder of the yacht or broker without first checking on alternative sources. The salesman or broker concerned is probably entitled to commission on any deal he makes, and may be inclined to offer inducements which would not stand up to close examination.

8. Carefully check the true interest rate to be charged. Depending upon the amount and period of the loan a seemingly attractive 8 or 9% can amount to 20% or more when expressed as a true rate. Official tables for calculating the true rate of interest have been issued by the Office of Fair Trading and

are held by Trading Standards and Consumer Protection Departments. When the Consumer Credit Act is fully operational most of these problems will be taken care of, but in the interim caution is well advised.

Building Payments on new yachts are not deemed to be credit trading providing a clause exists in the contract by which ownership of the vessel and all gear and equipment appropriated to her passes to the buyer on each payment as discussed in Chapter 5. If the SBBNF form of contract is not used then the acceptance of building payments by a builder may be deemed to be credit trading and all the controls of the 1974 Act would be invoked.

10 Obtaining A Mooring

There was a time when a yachtsman seeking a mooring merely paid a few pounds a year to a harbour authority, local authority, or private owner of a river or estuary, sank his own mooring, and enjoyed security of tenure thereafter. Those halcyon days have gone, as they were bound to do, for there are quite simply too many yachtsmen seeking moorings in too little water. It was inevitable that large scale commercial development would be required to cater for the huge expansion of boating, and equally inevitable that costs would increase and the freedom of the yachtsman would decrease. Although it is still possible to obtain a swinging mooring in the more remote parts of the country, the fact is that most yachtsmen are obliged to go into a marina, or lie to commerically provided piles or trots. Even where a swinging mooring is available it is controlled by a harbour authority or commercial company and the yachtsman is obliged to enter into a formal agreement for his mooring.

Whether the owner and provider of the mooring is a public authority, a club, or a commercial company, the yachtsman is virtually obliged to take whatever is offered. The provision of moorings is a seller's market and will continue so for the forseeable future. It therefore follows that freedom to negotiate the most favourable contract is severely limited. It may be that a particular locality for a mooring is so important that one is obliged to grin and bear whatever terms are offered. On the other hand there are marinas and other commerical moorings which, although usually full, do have vacancies from time to time, and it is therefore possible to look around for the most favourable contract.

The activities of some marinas in imposing unfair conditions of contract on their customers has received much adverse publicity in the yachting press in recent years. As a result of this and of considerable efforts by the RYA, some of the worst excesses have disappeared, but there are still some thoroughly undesirable restrictions imposed on yachtsmen by a few companies. These take two forms. First, there are restrictions upon the yachtsman's freedom to sell his own vessel privately or through the broker of his choice, and secondly, there are restrictions on his freedom to work on his own vessel or to employ a contractor of his choice.

The justification offered by some marinas and yards for this state of affairs is that there is little or no profit from moorings and they rely on brokerage and being commissioned to do work on boats on their moorings to make up the loss. So ingrained into the thinking of the marine industry have such arguments become that even the RYA, the SBBNF, and the National Yacht Harbour Association give credence to them. It is indeed possible that there may be strength in the argument in regard to a few small yards which provide moorings as an adjunct to their normal business, but in the case of big marinas it is an utterly fatuous argument, and the profitability of those which do nothing but provide moorings proves the point. Ethical problems of this nature are quite common in an industry which has enjoyed a period of rapid growth, and in most cases the problem is no more than a state of mind which is the result of long established but outmoded practice. It is easy enough to think back a few years to a time when the norm was a small yard providing moorings for its customers. It would have been unthinkable for outside contractors to have come onto the premises of the yard to do work which could equally well have been done by the yard itself. But that is no longer the case, and there is now much discussion about how these practices can be removed or mitigated. Some progress has been made, but there is much to be done, and it is as well if the yachtsman seeking a mooring is aware of the problem.

Let us first consider the question of selling a boat which is berthed with a company placing restrictions on the freedom of the yachtsman to sell as he wishes. The form of such restriction varies enormously from a simple requirement that the owner should merely inform the harbour office of his intention to sell to something like the following:-

> *In the event that the owner wishes to sell his vessel whilst usually berthed and/or stored at the company's premises the company shall be notified in writing by the owner, and the company shall irrevocably be entitled as agent on behalf of the owner to appoint its brokerage concessionaires at the premises as sole agents for a period of 12 months from such appointment in the sale for the owner who shall pay to the said brokerage concessionaires commission at the following rates. . . . . .*

Other contracts do not go quite so far in that they do permit the owner to sell his vessel privately in addition to putting her in the hands of the brokerage concessionaires, providing that 1% or 2% of the price obtained on the private sale is paid over to the company. Yet others permit private sales without any restrictions on brokerage, but demand a percentage of the price.

The contract quoted above, which is still in use, is surely quite outrageous. It attempts to prevent a yachtsman from selling his own vessel privately, it gives the company sole rights through its brokers, to sell the vessel for a period of up to a year and collect the commission, and it prevents the owner from taking his vessel elsewhere to sell it, with the obvious implication that he will lose his berth if he does so. The other forms of contract mentioned are less objectionable, but it is only a matter of degree. There can be no justification for using the shortage of moorings to penalise yachtsmen in this way. Fortunately the passing of the Fair Trading Act and the appointment of the Director General of Fair Trading brought a breath of fresh air into this unhealthy situation. The Act gives the Director General far reaching responsibilities for action on restrictive agreements relating to services, of which the provision of moorings is one. The Act requires the Director General to call in contracts of service for examination and possible registration, and as soon as this was done there was much thought given by the various trade associations and marina companies as to their position. In 1975 a new set of General Regulations and Conditions of Berthing in Marinas and yacht harbours was agreed jointly by the National Yacht Harbour Association and the RYA. The relevant clause in respect of sales in the new regulations was as follows:-

> *The owner shall be permitted to arrange a private sale of not more than one vessel . . . . . . during one or more periods of 12 consecutive months of the licence granted to the owner. In the event of such private sales: (1) The owner shall be present at all times during which the vessel is to be viewed, and he shall not be permitted to display a 'For Sale' notice on his vessel whilst at the company's premises; (2) The owner shall not be required to pay commission to the company upon such private sale in excess of one percent of the sale price except where prior notice has been given by the company of a higher rate of commission.*

The removal of the restriction on private sales was very welcome, but the objections to payment of commission remained.

Since 1975 discussion of this problem has continued and much to their credit more and more marinas have removed all restrictions on the private sale of boats on their premises. Two of the largest marinas on the South Coast, which have earned a well deserved reputation for good business and modest charges, have done just this, and have even gone so far as to permit owners to put 'for sale' notices on their vessels. It is to be noted that brokers with offices within these marinas have not apparently suffered any adverse effects from these new arrangements and express their condemnation of the practice of seeking commission on private sales in forthright terms.

However, there are circumstances where charges on private sales may be justified. If the private seller allows potential buyers to go to the marina to inspect the vessel unaccompanied, then marina staff may well be involved in giving directions or closing up a yacht after inspection. Costs will be incurred and it is therefore entirely reasonable that owners should either be required to be present at all times, or a charge should be made. It must also be appreciated that there are a growing number of small dealers in boats who attempt to use marina facilities for their business without making any payment to the marina company. In such cases it is reasonable that a charge should be made. The problem really arises because of the use of the term "commission" because in such cases we are really talking about "access money".

Clearly this is a difficult problem and the author has made extensive enquiries of leading figures in the industry to test opinion. The general view seems to be that whilst they do not care for such charges in respect of genuine private sales by yachtsmen who only change their boats every three to five years or less, they do wish to see some control over the part time dealer and the careless or unscrupulous private seller. That is perfectly understandable, and any private yachtsman who has such a clause in his mooring agreement, and wishes to sell privately would be well advised to discuss the matter openly with the marina management. He may find that they are willing to waive the charge.

In recent years, however, another undesirable practice has grown up with a small minority of yacht harbours or marinas. Whilst placing no restrictions on private sales, they refuse to allow any broker other than their own concessionaires to have dealings with boats on their moorings. This is a restrictive trade practice which may well be illegal, and does the industry no credit.

Restrictions on the right of the owner to work on his own vessel or to permit outside contractors to do so are also common. A typical clause in marina contracts of a few years ago, which may still be found occasionally today, was:-

> *Except as hereinafter mentioned no owner shall undertake or permit any other person to undertake the painting of the top sides and/or bottom of his vessel on the premises. The owner or his permanent crew shall be permitted*

> *to touch up paint work on the topsides of his vessel provided (1) no damage is caused to the premises and (2) no nuisance or annoyance is caused to other users of the premises.*
>
> *No repair work shall be done on the vessel whilst at the company's premises (unless with the written consent of the company) other than minor running repairs of a routine nature by the owner or his permanent crew not causing any nuisance or annoyance to any other users of the premises.*

This clause amounts to an obsolute prohibition on all work in the marina or harbour without the written consent of the company. Most of those who use this clause have their own or an associate company's yard on the premises and insist on all work being done by that yard. Other companies are yet more specific and actually name the yard by whom all work is to be done in the mooring contract.

Although the above clause is just about the most restrictive of all those in use, many companies with the support and approval of the SBBNF and the NYHA and with the blessing of the RYA use clauses such as:-

> *Our permission must be obtained for the employment of any contractor and/or persons other than the permanent crew of the owner to undertake work on any vessel and/or gear on our premises or while afloat on any of our moorings.*

This clause is obviously much fairer if permission is not unreasonably withheld. It does, for example, permit the owner to do his own work and thus the fundamental objection to earlier clauses is removed. Sometimes permission to use outside contractors is withheld for valid reasons, such as the employment of difficult or unreasonable contractors, the use of outside firms or individuals who do not have the same overheads and costs as the yard, or the use of outsiders who use warranty work on new vessels to poach business from the resident yard's premises. The growth of 'bagmen' in the trade who use marina and yard facilities whilst charging no VAT and paying no tax is clearly unfair to established business and cannot be permitted.

These are difficult problems which are still under discussion between the SBBNF, the RYA and the Office of Fair Trading. There will have to be a compromise between the ideal of total and free competition, and the need to ensure that unscrupulous elements in the industry do not use marina and harbour facilities unfairly.

Meanwhile, it is wise to ask to see a copy of the contract before agreeing to take a mooring. If there are restrictive clauses in it, try to find a company which does not impose such restrictions. It may be wise to go to one of the good marinas where there are no restrictions other than those approved by

SBBNF and the RYA. Although the mooring fees may be higher than others it could be cheaper in the long run than paying commission on private sales and being obliged to employ an inefficient or excessively costly yard.

It is always worth discussing such problems with the dockmaster and yard manager. It may be that the company is merely seeking to protect itself against rogues and will be quite willing to give consent upon reasonable request.

11 False Trade Descriptions

The Trade Descriptions Act, 1968 is a criminal law statute and, by itself, can do nothing for the individual consumer. Its purpose is to protect the public generally against false and misleading descriptions of goods and services. The Act has been widely misunderstood, and most people expect it to provide solutions to problems which are outside its scope. A priest once quite seriously enquired whether his promises of a life hereafter could, if found to be unfulfilled, constitute an offence against the Act!

A false trade description is an untruth uttered about goods which are offered for sale to the public. The 'untruth' does not have to be made intentionally, for the law creates what is known as an 'absolute offence'. The mere statement of the falsehood constitutes the offence even if the person or company who make the statement, or someone else who merely repeats the statement, are unaware that it is false. The Act, in common with most other consumer protection laws, expects tradespeople to know their business and to be able to identify false or misleading statements about the goods they sell. There are some statutory defences built into the Act to remove undue harshness from the 'absolute offence' concept, but in the main, any tradesman or businessman who sells or offers anything for sale to which a false trade description has been applied is guilty of an offence.

A false trade description can be applied in a variety of ways. It can be a statement on a label, in an advertisement, or on a display card, or it can be applied by word of mouth. It is even possible to apply a false trade description without saying or doing anything, that is, by implication. If, for example, a yachtsman went into a chandlers' shop and asked for a tube of caulking compound suitable for the seams of a teak-laid deck and was merely handed something by the chandler without comment, that chandler would be deemed to have applied a trade description to that tube to the effect that it was suitable for caulking a teak-laid deck. If it proved to be unsuitable then he would have applied a false trade description for which he could be prosecuted.

A false statement must be false to a 'material degree' to constitute an offence. As to what is a material degree is a matter for the courts to decide in each case, but generally speaking the false description must be of some significance. It must materially affect the pocket, general welfare or physical safety of the buyer. This term is put into the Act to stop frivolous prosecutions over, for example, the 'whiter than white' detergent advertisements. Nobody takes the claims of such advertisements seriously and they are generally accepted as being silly but harmless. Similarly it would, perhaps not be a false trade description to refer to a yacht as being a 'fine vessel' because such a description is too vague to mean very much, but on the other hand there have been prosecutions where an object has been described as being a 'perfect example' because that is a more precise statement about condition.

The Trade Descriptions Act applies only to persons in trade or business, and thus a private yachtsman selling his own craft cannot commit an offence no matter how outrageous may be the claims he makes for his vessel. But he should be careful, for the provisions of the Misrepresentation Act, 1967 do apply and he could be sued at civil law. A broker is in trade or business and any statements he makes about a vessel offered for sale could land him in court. The Act applies to all manufacturers of marine equipment, the builders of boats, chandlers, brokers, yacht charter companies, and all others who earn money from the industry.

False or misleading indications of price are covered by the Act. There are two main points here. First, it is an offence to give a misleading indication of reduced price. Thus a 'flash offer' on cans of paint, that they have been reduced from £1.85 to £1.25 when in fact they never were sold at the original price of £1.85 is an offence. Secondly, it is an offence to charge a higher price for goods than that indicated. For example if echo sounders are advertised at a price of £145, but when a potential customer enquires he is told that he must pay £155, an offence has been committed. These provisions are often mistakenly thought of as a system of price controls. They are not. There are no price controls on marine equipment or services. The 1968 Act merely attempts to prevent misleading pricing.

Services are covered by the Act to the extent that it is an offence to wilfully or recklessly make a statement about the provision of those services. Wilfully means that the misrepresentation was deliberate, and recklessly means that the statement was made carelessly and without proper regard for its truth. Thus if a yard was contracted to carry out a refit on a yacht and on completion of the job charged for the full extent of the work, and it was subsequently found that they had omitted to do certain important parts of it, then they would be guilty of making a reckless statement about the service they had provided.

There is an important feature about these offences, however, which is not always appreciated. It is not an offence simply to be inefficient. Thus if a yard had agreed to complete a job by a certain time and failed to do so, it would be necessary to prove beyond reasonable doubt that they knew they could not finish it on time when they agreed to take on the work. That would clearly be impossible in the majority of cases. There is much discussion about the need to strengthen the Act to make it an offence to fail to do what has been agreed, but there are difficulties about this. We are all inefficient from time to time and to make it a criminal offence to err in this way seems to many observers to be taking consumer protection too far. It is always possible to sue in the civil courts if an inefficient firm has occasioned loss to its customers.

Nevertheless the section of the Act dealing with services is an important piece of protection for yachtsmen. Jobs not properly completed are fairly common, and if a contractor confirms that he has done all the work ordered but in fact has failed to do it, then he would be held to be guilty of an offence. In essence we are back to what we discussed in chapter 3; if the full extent of the work required is not put into an enforceable contract then there is no possibility of prosecution under the Trade Descriptions Act nor action at civil law.

The sale of short weight or measure in fuel, lubricating oil, rope, paint, and the many other things bought by yachtsmen by weight and measure is an offence under the Trade Descriptions Act, and the Weights and Measures Act, 1963. If a container states a quantity on a label, as most goods are required to do, and there is a lesser amount in the container, then an offence has been committed. If a yachtsman gives an order for so many litres of fuel and a lesser amount is delivered, then an offence is committed, and so on.

Responsibility for the enforcement of the Trade Descriptions Act and the Weights and Measures Act rests on County Councils in England and Wales, Regional Councils in Scotland, and the London Boroughs in London. To a very large extent they rely on complaints from the public as an aid to enforcement, and any yachtsman who believes that an offence has been committed is entitled to take his complaint to the Trading Standards or Consumer Protection department of the authority in whose area the offence has been committed. In the main this means the place at which the customer bought the goods or where he first became aware of the false description. In the case of mail order goods the place of offence would be at the recipient's home. Any department will, of course, advise as to where a complaint should be taken.

The decision as to whether a prosecution is to be taken by the local authority rests with them alone. No member of the public has the right to insist on a case being taken, but the authority is under a statutory obligation to efficiently investigate complaints and if any ratepayer believes that an authority is falling down on its job he can complain to his local councillor. The Commissioner for Local Administration (the Ombudsman) can look into a complaint about lack of investigation of an offence, but he cannot interfere with the decision to prosecute.

The Trade Descriptions Act allows for private prosecutions to be taken by ordinary citizens or firms. To the best of the author's knowledge only two such cases have been taken since the Act came into force and both failed. On the whole, if the local authority does not consider that there is a case worth taking then it is a fair bet that the private citizen would fail. The reasoning behind the legislators' decision to allow private prosecutions is a little obscure because the same facility does not exist under other consumer protection statutes. Since the Act itself can bring no recompense to the consumer the motive for a private prosecution must be punitive, and that perhaps, is not the best motive for litigation.

Although the Trade Descriptions Act can bring no redress for the consumer, it is possible, as we saw in chapter 1, for the prosecutor to apply for a *compensation order from the magistrates* after a conviction has been imposed by the court. It is a matter for the local authority prosecutor as to whether an application for an order should be put to the court, but he will not to do so unless the complainant wishes. The power for prosecutors of criminal law cases to apply to the courts for compensation orders for the victims of crimes was introduced in 1967 as a result of public concern about the plight of peoples who had been robbed, burgled, raped, assaulted, and so on. It was almost by chance that the new arrangements applied to prosecutions under the Trade Descriptions Act, and there were many lawyers who believed that they should not. However, many local authority prosecutors began to apply for compensation orders following trials under the Act, especially in relation to second hand motor cars. There is no reason why the same should not be done in relation to boats and equipment.

The arrangements for compensation orders by criminal courts bridged the traditional gap between criminal and civil law in the United Kingdom. Never before had criminal courts been able to award compensation to individuals, and there were some lawyers and clerks to courts who disapproved of it. Perhaps for this reason the response of the courts to applications for compensation vary enormously. A few will go the whole way and order compensation amounting to the full cost of the goods concerned, but others, perhaps nervous of their powers or unskilled in assessing the value of compensation, stop well short of the sums needed. The author has prosecuted many cases where his request for compensation has been met by the award of a token sum.

The award of an order for compensation does not prevent the complainant from taking further action in the civil courts, but clearly a compensation order for part of the claim followed by a further action in the county court for the balance is an untidy arrangement. It would be better to go for the full amount in the county court.

For these reasons the decision to apply for a compensation order to a magistrates's court should be considered carefully, but it is still well worth while to draw the attention of the local authority to breaches of the Trade Descriptions Act. Not only does it protect the public generally and raise the standard of ethical trading, but a conviction at criminal law means that any subsequent action in the civil courts is almost certain to succeed.

Fear of being called as witness in a court case deters many people from making a complaint to the local authority. This is perfectly understandable because attendance at court is time wasting and seldom pleasant. However, under a procedure introduced in 1971 the investigating officer can take a written statement from the complainant in a prescribed form and serve it with the summons on the defendant. It is then for the defendant to give notice to the prosecutor if he wishes the complainant to attend court to give evidence. If he does not give such notice the complainant need not attend, unless the court requests it, and his statement is merely read to the court. It is for the investigating officer to decide whether to use this procedure, but it is used in a majority of cases quite successfully.

12 When Things Go Wrong

In this chapter we deal with the remedies available to a yachtsman who has bought an article which is not fit for the purpose intended, is not of merchantable quality, or does not correspond to a description, or who has a breach of contract problem with a yard, a broker, or surveyor. Ultimately of course, the answer may lie in court action, but the vast majority of problems are resolved without court action by sensible negotiation between the aggrieved buyer and the vendor. We talk about actions in the courts in chapter 13. In this chapter we discuss the preliminary stage which, if handled skilfully, can often be the final stage too.

First we deal with goods which have failed the principles established by the Sale of Goods Act, 1893, as amended by the Supply of Goods (Implied Terms) Act, 1973. These principles are explained in chapter 2. It is worth repeating at this stage that the rights of the buyer relate to the retailer, that is the person or company from whom he bought the goods. If there is a manufacturers' guarantee then that is a separate contract between the buyer and the manufacturer. Nothing written in a manufacturers' guarantee can remove the legal rights of the buyer against the retailer, and the retailer cannot shift his responsibility onto the manufacturer.

Where a boat or piece of equipment has been bought which is not of merchantable quality, or not fit for the purpose intended, or does not correspond with a description, the buyer has a right to cancel the contract and demand his money back. If he wishes, he can accept some lesser remedy such as allowing the seller to replace the item with another, or he can allow the seller to repair the defective goods. The best remedy depends upon the problem. It may be that the goods are so defective that the buyer wants nothing more to do with them and is prepared only to accept his money back. On the other hand it may be that an item is simply a bad example of a normally perfectly good product which can be rectified to the satisfaction of the buyer.

As soon as the buyer becomes aware that the goods are defective and fail to meet one or more of the principles mentioned above, then he must take action. Unreasonable delay in pursuing his rights on the part of the buyer would not be looked on kindly by the courts.

The first step is to write to, or go to see the retailer concerned and calmly and politely tell him about the problem. Always ask to see someone in authority. Just how high up in the company one should go depends upon the size of the firm and the value of the goods, but generally speaking the shop assistant in a chandler's shop, or junior manager for a boat builder will have no authority to agree to a sensible solution to the problem. If the firm is a well managed one the matter will immediately be put right at this stage, but the offer of a credit note instead of a refund of money is not the answer. If the buyer wishes to agree to a credit note well and good, but he is not obliged to do so. In any event unless the buyer is willing to accept a replacement or a repair he must make it absolutely clear at the outset that he wishes to have his money back. Failure to do so could lose him this right.

As to just how long after purchase a complaint can be made is a very difficult question. It all depends upon the type of goods, their value, and how much use they have had. In dealing with questions like this the courts have to fall back on common sense and try to decide what the ordinary man would consider reasonable. If the goods do not correspond to a description, then it would be reasonable to expect this to become apparent very soon after purchase, and a complaint should be made very quickly. If the goods are not fit for the purpose this too should become apparent soon after they are put into use, and a complaint should be made quickly. But if it is alleged that the goods are not of merchantable quality it may well be that they did not fail until some time after purchase, and thus possible action by the purchaser would be delayed. In this case yet another complicating factor is introduced, because the goods may have been misused by the buyer and it is reasonable for the seller to want some reassurance on this point. This is particularly the case with marine equipment which is often complex in construction and used by relatively inexperienced yachtsmen. An engine manufacturer faced with a complaint from a buyer that an engine had broken down after one season's use might very well wonder if it had been properly serviced, and whether the fault had arisen because of misuse by the owner. In cases like this the buyer must expect the seller to want reassurance on these points, and he may find it necessary to produce some technical supporting evidence for his claim. It may be necessary, for example, to seek a report from a qualified marine engineer about the cause of the defect in an engine which has had some use since purchase.

If resistance is met after the first approach to the retailer, then it is necessary to plan subsequent steps carefully. Conversations and telephone calls are of little value if the problem should ultimately end up in court, and so it is necessary to put everything into writing and to keep copies. The first point to establish is that the goods were actually purchased from the retailer to whom the complaint is addressed, and an invoice or returned cheque is the best possible proof. If the invoice, receipt, or other document received at the time of purchase has been lost, it is necessary to get the retailer to agree that the goods were in fact purchased from him. He cannot be blamed for asking for assurance on this point for there is, regrettably, a growing army of consumers who will fabricate cases to obtain money refunds.

Having established evidence that the goods were purchased from the firm to whom the complaint is made, it is then necessary to write a formal letter setting out details of the problem. In the absence of a known individual in a senior position in the company the letter should always be addressed to the 'Company Secretary' in the case of a limited company, or to the proprietor personally in the case of a private trader or partnership. It is very easy at this stage to make a near fatal mistake by simply writing a general sort of letter setting out the problem in conversational terms and expressing the hope that the seller will put it right. Such a letter contains a legal implication that the buyer is willing to accept a remedy suggested by the seller and is not insisting on his ultimate right to have his money back. It is therefore necessary at the outset to state that the contract is deemed to be void and the buyer wants his money back, but some other solution might be acceptable. A suggested form of letter is shown in Appendix C. Above all, deal only with the facts, keep the letter polite but formal, and avoid emotion. Such phrases as "your dreadful piece of equipment spoiled our holiday to which we had been looking forward for so long. My wife and I will never forgive you", do nothing for the case and may serve to convince the seller that he is dealing with a fool.

After sending the letter wait for a period of fourteen days as mentioned in the draft (appendix C) and if a negative reply, or no reply at all, is received move at once to the next step. It is here that advice as to the strength of the case and how to proceed may be of assistance. If it is a simple case, such as a life jacket which will not inflate, then no help is needed for the fault is obvious. But if some more complex equipment is involved, or if the buyer is unsure as to just how hard to press his case, he may feel the need for some support or encouragement. Some sources of help are discussed below with frank assessment based on the author's own experience of each.

Solicitors

If the case involves goods of less than £200 value there is little point in seeking the help of a solicitor as his costs are likely to be too high to make it worth while to employ him. In any case it is possible to deal with small cases under the arbitration procedures of the County Court (chapter 13) without a solicitor. In cases involving sums in excess of £200 the use of a good solicitor is sometimes helpful, but it is still possible to handle the matter alone. If the case concerns sums in excess of £2,000 then the use of a solicitor is essential because actions cannot be taken in the high court without proper legal representation. It is, however, important to find a solicitor who is knowledgeable in marine matters. It must be realised that solicitors deal with the whole spectrum of law and a general practicing solicitor who earns most of his income from conveyancing, and matters of probate and divorce, is likely to be out of his depth in marine matters, even though he may have a good grasp of the basics of contract law. The best solution to a problem often requires a knowledge of the industry, of the goods concerned, and of the various trade associations which may be able to help. Some firms of solicitors do specialise, and it is worth seeking the services of one who may have had marine law experience and specialises in civil actions.

Consumer Advice Centres

There are about 75 full blown consumer advice centres, mainly in London and the big cities operated by local authorities or the Consumers Association, together with many trading standards offices where consumer advice is available. They vary enormously in competence, but most of them are able to give advice on civil law and arbitration schemes. The advice is free, but its quality is often not what it should be.

Citizens Advice Bureaux

There are more than 800 CABs situated all over the country which can give general advice on consumer law, legal aid, and court actions. Some of them have 'legal surgeries' at which solicitors attend on a rota basis to advise on consumer problems. It is usually necessary to make an appointment for such an interview. Advice is free, but the bureaux naturally have little experience of marine matters.

Arbitration Schemes

Where a contract contains an arbitration procedure, such as in the case of the SBBNF contract on new vessels, it is well worth trying. Arbitration is an established way of resolving disputes in the marine industries and often provides a quick, cheap, and fair solution. A small fee is required to set up the enquiry which is returnable if the complaint is upheld.

A Surveyor or Engineer

If help needed is merely confirmation that the complaint is a valid one and guidance as to the value of the claim, then it is worth while seeking the advice of a surveyor or an engineer. The problem may well require an inspection for which a fee will be payable, but this is a good investment if it is the difference between presenting a good case or an ill prepared one. In any case, if the action is successful the costs can be recovered.

Once it is decided that there is a good case worth fighting a further letter should be sent to the retailer, and a suitable form, depending upon the circumstances, might be that in Appendix D. Note that the letter informs the seller that the goods are available for his inspection. It would be wrong to release the goods to him because the evidence would then be lost if it should prove necessary to take the matter to court. On the other hand he must be given a chance to check that the claim is a genuine one. But once it has been established beyond doubt that the goods are defective and technical evidence is available to that end, then there would be no harm in releasing them to the other party on receipt of a letter from them giving assurance that they would be returned in time for production in court if that should prove to be necessary.

If an unsatisfactory reply or no reply at all is received to the second letter then court proceedings should be started without delay. We explain how this should be done in chapter 13.

If the seller does offer to put the matter right on receipt of the second letter, as is often the case, it is sometimes necessary to consider whether to compromise or to proceed for the full claim. If the offer from the other side goes most of the way, but still leaves a small sum outstanding the decision can be a difficult one. Consequential costs such as that for the fitting and/or removal of an appliance from a yacht should also be claimed. If an offer of a full refund for the cost of the goods is received but not for the consequential costs, it is a matter of judgement as to whether it is worth pressing on with the full claim. If fitting costs or other out of pocket expenses are small it is probably wise to settle, but if they are substantial such as the cost of removing and re-fitting an engine, the full claim should be pressed home.

Next we deal with a breach of contract on services which can be anything from work not properly carried out by a yard to failure of a broker to fulfill his obligations, or a dispute with a marina. The range of possible cases facing a yachtsman in this field is enormous, and the remedies, despite all we have said in previous chapters, are less well defined than in the case of goods. Where goods are supplied in the course of a contract of service, the remedies under Sale of Goods law apply to them. Where the problem is one of work being done inadequately or not at all, or a failure to carry out a general responsibility under a contract, it is necessary to admit that the point at which it becomes worth while to proceed with court action is very difficult to determine. This is partly because the legal rules are less well defined, and also partly because the monentary value of that section of the contract not satisfactorily discharged is difficult to assess.

The decision to take action over a breach of contract when the work has not been done at all is a simple one. On the other hand, it may be that in the opinion of the yachtsman a job has not been done very effectively. In such cases a second opinion is well worth having, and if the case involves a significant monetary value then the opinion of a surveyor or engineer is essential. Many experienced yachtsmen feel, with much justification, that their knowledge is as good as that of a surveyor in many matters, but they should appreciate that a court can hardly be blamed for preferring the views of one who has no financial interest in the outcome of a case. Similarly, the other party to a dispute over a breach of contract is far more likely to be willing to settle out of court if the evidence is confirmed by an independent and expert opinion.

The procedure for dealing with a breach of contract of service is much the same as that described earlier in this chapter for goods. Once it has been decided that there is a breach of an enforceable contract, with documentary evidence available in the form of written instructions to the contractor, then the letter suggested in appendix C, suitably amended, may be sent if the account for the work has been paid. If payment has not been made when the breach of contract is discovered the yachtsman can negotiate from a position of strength for a proper completion of the work or a reduction in price.

When all efforts to reach a negotiated settlement have been exhausted it is then necessary to take the decision to go to law. The procedure is described in the next chapter, but it is important to ensure that there is no possibility of a settlement first. The courts do not take kindly to precipitate actions, but on the other hand it is unwise to dither over legal action once it becomes clear that the other side have no intention of fulfilling their obligations.

13 Going To Court

The action following a decision to go to court depends upon the sum involved. If it does not exceed £200 action may be under the small claims or arbitration procedure in the County Court. If it is between £200 and £2000 it may be by normal trial in the County Court, and if it exceeds £2,000 it must be in the Queen's Bench Division of the High Court. In the latter case legal representation is essential, and since this book is of a 'do it yourself' nature we will not discuss the procedures involved in respect of High Court Actions. However, it is wise to bear in mind that if the claim is for a sum only a little more than £2,000 it might be wise to reduce it to one of £2,000 and proceed in the County Court. The proceedings would be over more quickly and the costs in the event of failure would be greatly reduced. In any case of this magnitude the advice of a good solicitor should be heeded.

The County Courts were created in the mid-nineteenth century to try civil cases on a local basis involving small sums of money. There are more than 300 County Courts in the United Kingdom, situated in towns and cities, but there is no logical pattern. They are not, for example, based upon local authority boundaries. They are, however, divided into 60 districts, and in charge of the judicial proceedings in each district is a County Court Judge. He is assisted by a Registrar who enjoys powers to try lesser cases in his own right.

The procedures in the County Courts are relatively informal since they exist to deal with small matters and have not developed the strict procedural rules which exist in superior civil courts and all criminal courts. In most County Courts the proceedings are conducted in an informal and relaxed atmosphere. Although the quality and style of each court depends to a large extent upon the personality of the registrar, who is the key figure in the system, most people who go to a County Court for the first time are agreeably surprised by its thoroughness and efficiency.

It is necessary at an early stage to decide whether to employ a solicitor for an action in the County Court. For actions under the small claims procedure it is, on the whole, unwise to use one for, as we have said, his costs are likely to be too high in relation to the sum claimed, to justify his employment. Indeed, the whole small claims procedure was set up in 1971 with the deliberate intention of providing a means of settling minor matters quickly and without legal representation. For sums in excess of £200 the trial is normally under the ordinary court procedures and the small claims procedures cannot be used unless both parties agree and the registrar so directs. A full trial in the County Court is well within the capability of the ordinary yachtsman who has a reasonable capacity to express himself coherently. The decision whether or not to employ a solicitor really depends upon the complexity of the case, and the ability of the complainant to handle the case himself.

If it is decided to employ a solicitor care should be taken in the selection of the right man. A local solicitor who knows the district where the problem arose and is familiar with the local County Court might be the best man in minor matters, but for High Court Actions it is better to seek the services of a skilled solicitor from one of the large practices in London where specialist knowledge of marine disputes is available. This is even more the case where it is necessary to instruct Counsel. Good solicitors tend to brief good counsel.

Before a summons can be issued for a hearing in the County Court it is important to ensure that the name appearing on the 'particulars of claim form' which is the form to be completed by the complainant for submission to the court office, is the right name of the defendant. If the suit is against a one man business and his name is known to the complainant all is well. It may be necessary to check on his full name as it appears on the register of electors at the local Town Hall, but no more is required. If the defendant is to be a limited company, easily identifiable by the abbreviation 'Ltd' or the full word 'Limited' after its name, then it is necessary to enquire about the correct registered office for insertion on the particulars of claim form. If there has been correspondence with the company and the full name and registered office appear on their note paper, then it is safe to use that name and address. Most large companies have their own registered office, but many small companies in the marine industry use the office of a local accountant as their registered office. That does not matter so long as the right address is given. If there is any doubt about the correct address confirmation may be obtained by a personal visit to The Companies

Registry, Companies House, Crown Way, Maindy, Cardiff, CF4 3HO on payment of a nominal search fee of 5p. In most cases, of course, a personal visit to Cardiff is out of the question, but there are a number of firms offering a companies search service on payment of modest fees. The best one to use depends, to some extent, on where the enquirer resides, but names and addresses of such firms are obtainable from Citizens Advice Bureaux and local authority trading standards departments, or in the Yellow Pages of the telephone directory under 'Company Agents'. It may be that the firm with whom the complainant has been dealing and wishes to sue is a partnership of two or more people who are either trading under their own names such as, Grey and Brown Marine Equipment, or who are using a business name such as Upper Creek Marine Equipment. In this latter case the name should be registered at the Registry of Business names at Pembroke House, 40-56 City Road, London EC1Y 2DN, and it is possible to find out the names and addresses of the responsible people through one of the 'company agents' mentioned above. It used to be possible for private citizens to make enquiries directly at both the Registry of Companies and the Registry of Business names. Unfortunately the service has been discontinued.

Armed now with all the information needed for a successful action, it is necessary to decide whether to apply to the County Court Office for a hearing under the small claims or arbitration scheme, or to go for a full trial. If the sum is less than £200 it is far better to ask for the matter to be dealt with by arbitration. In most cases the office will agree, and will then set the wheels in motion. It is still possible for the hearing to be under the arbitration scheme even if the amount is over £200, subject to the agreement of the other party and the registrar. This is a matter to be discussed with the court clerk when starting proceedings. If the sum sought is only just over £200 it is possible that the court clerk will suggest that it be reduced to £200 and taken by arbitration. That is a matter for the complainant to decide. He is not obliged to reduce his claim merely to make life easy for the court staff.

The arbitration scheme has now been running for some years and in most County Courts it works well. Unhappily, in a minority of courts the registrar or the judge is hostile to the scheme and the court clerks actively try to discourage its use. Curiously the main yachting centres in the United Kingdom have the best and the worst of the county courts known to the author. Any citizen who experiences discouragement or lack of courtesy from a county court should write and complain to the office of the Lord Chancellor.

It is important to start proceedings in the right court. Every complainant has the right to choose either the court in the area where he resides or carries on business, or the area in which the cause of the action occurred. In the case of defective goods bought at a marina shop on the South Coast by a yachtsman living in London, for example, the buyer would have the choice of taking proceedings at the court nearest to his home or the one nearest to the marina. In order to avoid one of the 'bad courts' it is sometimes worth while to contact the local Citizens' Advice Bureau or trading standards department and ask them what their experiences of the county court are.

To start an action in the County Court it is necessary to call at the court office and fill in a form known as a 'request'. This is an application for the court to hear the case, and must contain all the relevant information as to the identity of the 'defendant' or the 'respondent' as he is sometimes known, and the facts of the case. The court clerk will be willing to help in the completion of the form, but if advice is being sought elsewhere, then the form can be taken away and returned on completion.

A fee is payable to the court clerk to start the action. At the time of writing the fees are thought to be under review, but they are likely to be about £5 for a £100 claim, £7.50 for a £200 claim and so on. There is an additional fee of 50p for the costs of the court bailiff in serving the summons on the defendant. If the case is successful the defendant will be ordered to pay the costs of the complainant.

After checking the details of the case the court will prepare a summons for service and the complainant will be given a 'plaint note' which acts as a receipt for the fee and contains the case number. The case number is important because all documents relative to the case will be filed under that number.

Together with the summons a form of admission will be served on the defendant which he can complete with an offer of payment if he admits the claim submitted by the complainant. If he does not admit the claim, then the court will set down a date for the hearing of the case and both parties will be informed and ordered to attend. If the defendant fails to attend or respond he will, in most cases, have judgement entered against him. If the complainant fails to attend without good cause his case will be lost and he will have to pay his own costs and those of the other party.

The pre-trial review was an important new innovation in county court procedures introduced in 1971. Both parties to the case are invited to attend an informal interview with the Registrar who will go through the documents, and then see if there is any common ground between the two parties on which a settlement can be agreed. If a settlement is possible, the registrar will help the parties come to an agreement, and that is an end of the matter. If agreement is not possible, the registrar will discuss the way in which the case is to be handled and seek clarification of any doubtful points. He will also determine at this point if the case is to be dealt with by arbitration or full trial.

The arbitration procedure is a simple one. The normal laws of evidence which apply at a full trial are waived as far as is consistent with justice and an arbitrator, appointed by the registrar, will hear the case. The registrar often acts as the arbitrator himself, but may seek expert help in technical matters. The court can only decide to use the arbitration procedure if one party to the dispute requests it, and can only insist on it against the wishes of the other party in cases not exceeding £200. In cases above that amount it can only be done with the agreement of both parties.

There are two most important differences between the arbitration procedure and a normal trial. There are no appeals possible in arbitration unless in exceptional cases the registrar directs that there should be, and arbitration hearings are in private without the right of public attendance that applies in normal county court cases. This means that arbitrations are not reported in the local press.

Agreement on costs of replacement parts, repairs, or work not done is often possible once the summons has been served, either as a part of the pre-trial review or by private agreement between the parties. Private agreement is not likely where the complainant is taking his own case, but where both parties are represented by solicitors it is quite usual for them to agree on such things. Such agreements reduce the need for expert witnesses, thus reducing costs, and speeding up the trial.

Once the date of the hearing is fixed it can be changed by request to the court office if the reasons are valid, such as sickness, bereavement and so on. But if the other party to the dispute is put to additional cost because of the adjournment then the person seeking it may have to meet the extra costs.

Where an expert witness is to be used to support a case it is important that he puts his evidence into a written statement which can be produced to the registrar at the pre-trial review. A surveyor's report may well be accepted by both parties at the pre-trial review, thus removing the need for the surveyor to attend the hearing. It is important to tell experts that they may be needed in court before allowing them to proceed with any work. Although it is possible to compel reluctant witnesses to attend court, it is obviously much better if they do so willingly. It should also be realised that the Judge, Registrar, or Arbitrator is most unlikely to have any understanding of marine equipment or yachts. It would therefore be helpful, and no doubt much appreciated by the court, to take to the hearing either the equipment itself or some explanatory material. Some articles in the yachting press are excellent for explaining such things as the functioning of an engine, an echo sounder, a windlass, the heads, and many other things.

If attending a County Court for the first time it is a good idea to arrive early or to drop in at some previous time to sit and listen. The public are allowed to attend all hearings except those in arbitration, and it is surprising how quickly one gets the general idea of how the system works, and how soon a feeling of confidence is gained.

In cases where a solicitor is not being employed it is always possible to take someone along to assist the complainant. It may be a friend or colleague, and he or she may, with the consent of the registrar, speak for the complainant, although the complainant will inevitably have to give evidence.

During the hearing it may be necessary to be cross examined, that is to be asked questions by the other side on evidence given. It may also be necessary to ask questions of witnesses for the other side. This is necessary to clarify points of doubt, or to rebut misleading evidence which may have been given. In an arbitration hearing this is all very informal and the arbitrator will be very much in charge. In a full trial the judge supervises the proceedings. The tension associated with cross examination in fictional court room dramas does not occur in the County Court. It is all a very restrained and civilized procedure.

Judgement may be given immediately after the end of the case or it may be reserved until another date when the parties will be asked to return to hear it. Judgement is often reserved when the case is a complex one and the Judge or Registrar wishes to have time to consider all the problems involved. Once judgement is given there is a right of appeal by either party if it is thought unfair or unjust. The right of appeal in arbitration cases is limited to certain grounds of wrongful procedure which are very unlikely to arise. The right of appeal to a higher court following a full trial in the County Court would be explained by the court officials, but any litigant reaching the point where he feels that an appeal is necessary should seek qualified legal advice.

Costs, such as witness expenses and court expenses are usually awarded to the successful party to the proceedings and against the other party.

There is one crucial question to be asked before beginning any proceedings in the County Court. Could the defendant pay if the case is won? There is little point in achieving a successful case in the court if the other party has no money to pay. This is one of the dangers of doing business with very small firms who have little in the way of assets. If they are sued and go bankrupt the successful litigant merely becomes a creditor of the bankrupt business, and there is little satisfaction in that.

This problem contains an essential message for every yachtsman. The many unskilled bodgers who abound in the yachting world are simply not worth employing. They are not likely to do a good job, and when trouble arises the legal remedies open to the yachtsman are likely to amount to nothing.

14 Some Case Studies

To put some flesh on the bones of consumer protection outlined in previous chapters there is no better way than to talk about a few actual cases and discuss how they could be resolved. The following are all based on fact, but the events and the outcome have been altered to some extent to bring out the various principles we have discussed in this book.

Case 1. A man bought a motor sailer built in GRP by a continental company. He was the third owner, and had taken every reasonable precaution on buying. A reputable surveyor gave a generally favourable report and the buyer paid the £12,000 asking price, confident that he had a boat built to last for many years. At the end of the first season he had the vessel lifted out, and whilst scraping off some loose paint below the water line he discovered blisters in the gel coat. The further he went, the worse things became. The blisters could be scraped off leaving deep cavities in the GRP all over the bottom of the yacht.

The owner had a different surveyor look at the yacht who said that it was a severe case of osmosis. Due to a defective moulding, water had seeped into the pores of the mat and had gradually lifted off the gel coat. In his view the hull could never be satisfactorily repaired, and the yacht was unseaworthy.

The new owner contacted the second owner who, quite truthfully denied all knowledge of the problem, but gave the name and address of the first owner and promised all help. The first owner was contacted and he admitted that in the first two seasons a few affected places on the bottom of the hull had been found, but they had been expertly repaired. He denied all responsibility for not informing the second owner on the grounds that a survey had been done before sale.

The new owner wrote to the foreign manufacturers and the British importers. The former denied any responsibility saying that the problem must have been caused by lack of maintenance, and the latter simply said that they had no responsibilities to anyone other than the first owner.

The unfortunate buyer had no remedy. There was no misrepresentation by the seller who was genuinely unaware of the fault. The new owner had no contract with the builder or importer. His only possible action would be to sue the first surveyor he employed on grounds of negligence because he did not report the problem. The case actually occurred before the Unfair Contract Terms Act, 1977, and the surveyor could have relied upon a disclaimer in his report. If the problem arose today and the buyer could find a surveyor of equal or higher status than the first one, willing to state categorically that the faults could have been detected on a thorough survey, then it is possible that the first surveyor could be sued for damages.

The lesson?

Recognise the problem of osmosis in second hand GRP craft and instruct the surveyor in writing to look for it. Ask the previous owner in every case about the existence of blisters, discolourations, or holes on the gel coat, and appreciate the risks being taken in buying a second hand GRP boat.

Case 2. An inexperienced yachtsman prepared to make his first crossing of the English Channel. He forgot to get a weather forecast, and set out to find dense fog about half way across. He had not recorded his DR position at all, and had simply steered a compass course without allowance for tidal drift and leeway. He took out his new and unused radio direction finder, tuned into the beacon at his destination, and steered to that beacon under power. After six hours of motoring he put his yacht on rocks off the French coast some ten miles to the west of his destination. On returning home he had his RDF checked and found that it had a ten degree error in the compass.

The intrepid sailor went to his solicitor for advice who wrote to the manufacturers; they at once offered a refund of the price of the set or a replacement. They denied any liability for the damage to the yacht or the spoiled holiday.

The solicitor sought the advice of the author, who said that he thought the manufacturers were right. It was known to every competent sailor that RDF was an aid to good navigation and not an alternative to it. The courts would be likely to say that the yachtsman was negligent in not keeping a proper DR position, and in the absence of any claim by the manufacturers that the RDF could be used alone to navigate in fog, it was likely that a case would fail.

The yachtsman, after much huffing and puffing, finally accepted his solicitor's advice and accepted a replacement RDF set as full settlement of his claim. He spent the next winter at navigation classes.

The lesson?

There have been sufficient cases before the courts to show that a failure of equipment does not automatically result in liability for consequential damage for the manufacturer, if the skipper and crew could, by the use of proper seamanship, have mitigated or avoided the loss. That is the position in late 1978, but if current moves to overhaul the law on product liability come to fruition the position may be radically changed.

Case 3. A new yacht had been launched and was being taken under its own power to a berth in a marina when its steering gear failed. It was travelling at a considerable speed and its new owner was at the helm. It struck two other yachts, causing extensive damage. The owner had not completed his insurance arrangements, and at the time of the accident was not covered. Having signed the acceptance note the builder's insurance had lapsed.

The owners of the two damaged yachts claimed the cost of repairs to their vessels amounting to £550 from the new owner, and he in turn sought to claim all damages from the manufacturer of the steering gear when it was found that a Bowden cable had snapped. The manufacturers denied liability stating that the cable had broken because it had been incorrectly installed by the builders. The builders agreed to repair the broken steering gear, but declined responsibility for any of the damage to the yachts involved. They pointed out that the yacht had been moving too quickly in a confined space, and had she been moving at a slower speed it would have been possible to put her in reverse thus minimising damage.

The owner of the new yacht took advice from his solicitor who, having taken advice from a master mariner, suggested that a case would fail.

The lesson?

This case is similar to No. 2 and has been quoted to show the difficult problem surrounding product liability. There is an EEC Directive and a Law Commission Report which seek to introduce a system of strict and absolute product liability. Under the proposals the manufacturers of the RDF set and the steering gear, or perhaps the builder, could find themselves totally liable for all the damage concerned. This is, of course, speculation, but in the United States where a system of absolute product liability does operate there have been some curious reported cases. In one, which is reported as factual but cannot be vouched for, a woman is supposed to have successfully sued the manufacturer of a micro-wave oven because she put her dog in it to dry its coat and was surprised when it died. She sued on the grounds that the manufacturers should have put a notice on the oven stating that it was unsuitable for drying dogs! This is obviously a pretty far fetched case and it is unlikely that British courts would tolerate such foolishness, but if a system of absolute product liability is introduced into this country it will have profound effects on the marine industries. Yachtsmen will gain no satisfaction from it, for it will inevitably mean higher prices.

Case 4. A new engine was installed in an old yacht, and it was necessary to make extensive modifications to the engine bearers and the engine compartment to accommodate it. Soon after installation a connecting rod broke and fractured the engine casing. The owner was able to show that the engine had not been misused and had been properly serviced since installation. The builder contacted the manufacturer of the engine who agreed to replace it free of charge, but when the job was done the owner was surprised to receive a bill from the builders for the cost of removal of the damaged engine which had been greatly complicated by their own installation.

The lesson?

The owner was obliged to pay up because he was thought to have implied acceptance of the builder's arrangements with the manufacturer which were verbally communicated to him, because he had told the builders to proceed with the replacement without any agreement as to costs involved. His solicitor advised him that he would fail if he contested the bill for costs. At the time the author thought the advice of the solicitor was mistaken, but there was no doubt that the position of the owner would have been greatly strengthened if he had written to the builder immediately after the breakdown telling him that the engine was not of merchantable quality and rejecting the entire contract for installation. He could have made it clear that he expected the yacht to be returned to him with a good engine installed at no cost to himself. If the builder refused to do that he could have sued for the return of all his money and instructed another yard to do the job.

Case 5. A motor launch was hired which continually broke down and ruined an outing. The hirer sued the lessor and was successful, the court ruling that there is an implied undertaking in any contract of hire that the goods are fit for the purpose intended.

The lesson?

The case is an old one, but it contains a very important principle in the light of the growth of the yacht charter business. Many individual yachtsmen charter out their vessels for a part of the season and they should do all they can to ensure that the yacht is in good order and will not break down. If it does, they could face not only the full refund of the charter, but additional damages for loss of holiday, personal danger etc.

Case 6. In another hiring case, fire broke out in the vessel and it was found that there was no fire fighting equipment on board. Again the implied condition to the contract is that the vessel is fit for charter in every respect, and fully equipped to meet all likely hazards. Substantial damages were awarded.

The lesson?

This case confirms that fitness for purpose in respect of charter craft is a complex and difficult matter. There have been many other cases involving commercial vessels where it has been held that defects easily remedied by the crew did not make a vessel unseaworthy, but those which involved a major breakdown or a serious ommission of essential equipment did. The main point in all this is that there are many yachtsmen who go to sea in their own vessels without equipment which, by normal standards, would be regarded as essential. If they charter out their vessels in this condition they run grave risks.

Case 7. A small second hand motor cruiser was sold and was claimed to have a 1500 cc engine of a well known make. She was not surveyed and the buyer paid cash for her, to a broker who was acting for the vendor. The broker had advertised her as having a 1500 cc engine without checking the information he received from the owner. Soon after delivery the new owner was disappointed by her performance and consulted an engineer who told him that the engine was a smaller model from the same manufacturer, of 1100 cc's. It was difficult to tell them apart because they looked alike and the identifying plate on the rocker-cover was missing.

The buyer sought the advice of a consumer advice centre who passed the information to a trading standards office in the area where the broker had his office. It was rightly believed that the broker had committed an offence under the Trade Descriptions Act, 1968 in advertising the vessel as having a 1500 cc engine, and the broker would have had no defence if he had been charged because he took no precautions to check the information given to him by the owner. The local authority decided not to prosecute the broker, but advised the owner that he had a good case at civil law because there had been a misrepresentation as part of the contract.

The buyer took up the matter with the broker who, having been told by the trading standards officer that he was not to be prosecuted, was in truculent mood. He told the buyer that if he sued, the case would be defended to the hilt, and the buyer was nervous of proceeding further.

The lesson?
This was a strightforward case for which the law provides ample remedies. The buyer felt that almost anything was better than getting involved in court action. He was unwise for he would almost certainly have won. He should have rejected the contract on grounds of misrepresentation and demanded a full refund of his money. Worse still, the local authority in deciding not to prosecute, and the owner in deciding not to sue, encouraged an unscrupulous broker to further excesses at the expense of yachtsmen.

Case 8. A yacht, which had been put ashore for the winter in a yard, was accidentally knocked over on her side by a mobile crane owned by the yard. The yacht's owner was called to inspect the damage, and the yard manager assured him that it would be repaired at the yard's expense. After the repair was completed, and whilst fitting out for the next season, the owner noticed some deformation in the frames on the side where the damage had occurred. He called in a surveyor, who reported that there was extensive damage to the structure of the hull which had not been repaired. Estimates for the repair were in excess of £1,000. The yard claimed that they had put right all the damage done in the accident, and pointed out that they were not liable, because there was a notice prominently displayed in the yard, and a clause in their storage contract, which stated that they accepted no responsibility for loss or damage to any property whilst on their premises.

The owner took legal advice and was told that he could not sue the yard, for the disclaimer was a part of the contract he had with them. He was obliged to claim against his own insurance to pay for the damage.

The lesson?
This case took place before the Unfair Contract Terms Act, 1977 came into force. If it happened today the disclaimer of the yard would have effect only insofar as it was reasonable. Although the Act has not yet been tested in the courts in circumstances such as this, it is unlikely that the yard would be able to avoid liability. The yachtsman who suffers such an experience today could sue, with reasonable confidence of success.

Case 9. The owner of a traditionally built yacht laid his vessel up afloat, and in the spring asked the yard where she was berthed to lift her out, burn off and re-paint the hull, and generally fit her out for the season. There were no written instructions given, for he had done business with that yard for many years, and all his work had been done on the basis of verbal instruction. A few days later he received a telephone call from the yard manager to the effect that there was extensive ice-grazing of the planks around the water line. The strength of the planks had been affected to an extent which necessitated their removal and replacement. The owner was surprised, but on being assured that the job would not be too expensive told the yard to proceed.

When the bill arrived he was shattered. It was enormous and far beyond his expectations. He went to the yard and asked to see the removed planks, but was told that they had been destroyed. When he remonstrated over the size of the bill he got no satisfaction. He went to his solicitor who told him that he had no case and would have to pay up, unless he could show that the charges were grossly unfair in the light of the work done. In view of the fact that he had no evidence to show how bad the damage was, that was clearly impossible.

The lesson?
The owner was a foolish man. On being told of the damage he should have asked for a written report and a quotation for the work to be done. On receiving these he could, if unhappy about the amount to be charged, have had a surveyor look at the damage and advise about the costs of repair.

Case 10. A yachtsman bought a new sailing cruiser of well known foreign manufacture from a British importer, who was also a local broker. The yacht was delivered to the yard adjacent to the broker's office in mid-winter and left there for launching in the spring. In the spring he asked the yard to launch her, and was horrified to receive a telephone call from the manager to tell him that she had sunk.

It transpired that she had been lowered into the water by crane just before lunch, and when the men returned an hour later to rig her she had gone to the bottom. They lifted her out and found that a keel bolt was missing. She had simply filled through the hole where the bolt should have been.

The importer arranged for her to be dried out, and all damaged equipment was replaced, but although he was assured that all was well the owner had constant trouble. The interior joinery began to de-laminate, locker doors would not fit, interior linings came unstuck, and the boat was generally unsatisfactory. The owner naturally lost confidence in her, and when he eventually sold her he lost heavily because of her shabby condition and unhappy history.

The lesson?

The owner should have taken legal advice, and rejected the yacht on the grounds that she was not fit for the purpose intended on delivery to him, by virtue of the missing keel bolt. The fact that she had been in his legal ownership for three months before launching would have made no difference. To clinch his case he could have obtained the advice of a surveyor to the effect that the yacht had been totally immersed and would inevitably give trouble.

Appendix A

Suggested Form Of Contract For Private Sales Of Second Hand Yachts

AN AGREEMENT FOR THE SALE OF:

Name of Yacht

Registered Number (if any)

Port of Registry

Class

Tons Thames Measurement (if appropriate)

Date of Construction

By (name and address of vendor)

To (name and address of buyer)

Agreed Price (expressed in figures and words)

Terms of Agreement:-

1. Ten per cent of the agreed purchase price should be paid to the vendor at the time of signing this contract. This deposit is returnable if the buyer should wish to withdraw from this contract as a result of any material defect in the vessel or deficiency in her inventory which may be found by survey.

2. The purchaser may, at his own expense, haul up or place ashore and/or open up the yacht and its machinery for the purpose of inspection and/or survey. The said inspection and/or survey shall be completed within 14 days of the signing of this agreement, and in the event of the buyer wishing to withdraw from this agreement as a result of the said inspection and/or survey he shall make good damage caused by the surveyor, re-launch and close up the yacht as appropriate at his own expense.

3. Such defects and deficiencies as may be reported by the surveyor shall be discussed between the parties to this contract who may agree that the vendor shall correct them at his own expense or there shall be an agreed reduction in the purchase price to meet the cost of rectifying such defects, bearing in mind the age and value of the vessel. If such agreement is not reached this contract shall be void.

4. After the expiry of the period stated in clause 2 above the yacht shall be deemed to have been accepted by the purchaser and the balance of the purchase price shall be paid forthwith unless the purchaser, immediately after receiving the surveyor's report and not later than 7 days after the survey has been carried out, serves notice on the vendor that this contract is terminated. Such notice shall stipulate the material defects or deficiencies reported by the surveyor and which form the grounds for rejection of the yacht.

5. The purchaser, recognising that the vendor is a private seller and is not acting in the course of a trade or business, hereby accepts that all express or implied warranties or conditions statutory or otherwise are hereby excluded.

6. All notices given under this contract shall be in writing and shall either be delivered to the addressee personally, or shall be deemed to have been delivered after a lapse of forty eight hours from its posting by registered post or recorded delivery to his last known address in the United Kingdom or Republic of Ireland.

7. The vendor certifies that the yacht is free from encumbrances and that there are no liens current on her nor outstanding debts relative to her.

8. The vendor certifies that to the best of his knowledge and belief the yacht is free from defects, other than those pointed out to the buyer.

Signature of vendor .... Witness ....
Address ....
Occupation ....
Signature of purchaser .... Witness ....
Address ....
Occupation ....

Appendix B

Suggested Letter Of Instruction To A Broker To Accompany The Broker's Questionnaire In Commissioning The Sale Of A Second Hand Yacht

To:
Hard Tack Yacht Brokerage Ltd.,
Wajir Yacht Basin,
East Acton.

Dear Mr Scuppers,

I enclose herewith your completed questionnaire about my yacht 'Wagtail' together with a photograph as requested. I would be obliged if you would now find a buyer for me, and sell the vessel for about £ .... I confirm that the details of the vessel given in the questionnaire are correct, and that I have declared all defects in the yacht and her equipment as far as I am aware of them.

On completion of a sale to a purchaser introduced by you I agree to pay commission on the scale recommended by the current British Boating Industry Code of Practice. If you should be successful in finding a buyer I would wish to enter into an agreement for the sale with him in a form approved by the Royal Yachting Association.

I enclose the keys of 'Wagtail' in order that you may permit viewing of the yacht, but I would be obliged if you would ensure that all viewers are accompanied by a responsible person, and that the yacht is properly closed up after each inspection.

*In commissioning you to sell my yacht I agree to your being the Central Listing Broker in accordance with the conditions set out in your Central Listing Agreement/In commissioning you to sell my yacht I must inform you that I reserve my right to instruct other brokers or to sell privately as I deem appropriate.

Yours faithfully,

A. Hopeful

* (delete as appropriate – see chapter 7)

Appendix C

Draft Letter To A Retailer Concerning Goods Which Are Not Of Merchantable Quality, or Not Fit For The Purpose, etc.

By Registered Post or Recorded Delivery
Letter addressed to Company Secretary, Manager or Sole Proprietor as appropriate

Dear Sir,

On the .... *(date) I bought a* .... *(full description of the goods) from your premises at* .... *(full address of chandlery, yard etc) to which your invoice/receipt* .... *(number and date of document) refers.*

I now write to inform you that the goods are defective in that .... *(full description of fault) and in accordance with my rights under the Sale of Goods Act, 1893 as amended by the Supply of Goods (Implied Terms) Act, 1973 I hereby reject the goods. I must ask you for a full refund of the purchase price amounting to £* ....
together with the cost of fitting and removal from my yacht which amounts to £ ....
making a total claim of £ ....

However, WITHOUT PREJUDICE TO MY RIGHTS I am willing to accept a replacement/repair* providing this can be done without delay.

I would be pleased to receive your reply within 14 days of the date of this letter.

Yours faithfully,

A. Purchaser

*Delete as appropriate

The penultimate paragraph should only be included if the buyer is willing to accept a repair or replacement in lieu of a full refund. If a written reply is received promising a full refund/replacement on return of the goods to the shop this should be done. If a telephone call is received, do not return the goods and leave without the money. A promise that it will be sent on is not good enough, because the vital evidence of the defective goods will be lost.

Appendix D

Draft Letter For Use If An Unsatisfactory Reply, Or No Reply At All, Is Received In Response To The Letter In Appendix C

By Registered Post or Recorded Delivery
Letter Addressed to the Company Secretary, Manager, or Sole Proprietor as appropriate

Dear Sir,

With reference to my letter of .... *(date) I regret that I have received no reply/that your reply of* .... *(date) is unacceptable.**

In view of the fact that there is a clear breach of contract in that the goods were not of merchantable quality/not fit for the purpose intended/did not correspond with the description given* I have no alternative but to submit the facts to the County Court for adjudication. This will now be done and the appropriate documents will be served on you in due course.*

(The above paragraph to be used in respect of goods)

In view of the fact that there is a clear breach of contract in that you did fail to .... *(give details of work not done or improperly completed) I have no alternative but to submit the facts to the County Court for adjudication. This will now be done and the appropriate documents will be served on you in due course.**

Yours faithfully,

A. Purchaser

*Delete as appropriate

Index

	Page		Page
ABYA	40,49	Defective goods	11,15,78
Acceptance	34,43	- action	78
Access to vessels	33	- letters	79
Accident damage	59	Deposits	29
Actions in court	83	Descriptions	12
Advertisements	47		
Amateur building	45	Emergency repairs	24
Arbitrations	35,80,87	Enforcement of law	33,74
Balances of payments	43	False	
Bankruptcy	31	- to a material degree	73
Breach of contract	81	- trade descriptions	8,72
Brokers	38,40,49	- prices	73
Building instalments	30	- statements on services	73
Buyer's rights	11,77		
		Guarantees	12
Charter Companies	40		
Citizens Advice Bureaux	80	High Court	83
Civil Law	7,8	Hire purchase	60
Commission	51,53		
Construction delays	33,35	Inflation	23,32
Contracts	22	Injury	18
- definitions	11,14	Inspections	47
- disputes	35	Insurance	35
- enforcement	24	Insurance loans	61
- precise	27		
- service	17,20	Liens	26
- unfair terms	12,16,18	Loss of life	18
- verbal	19	Loss of vessels etc	18
- written	20,27,39		
Consumer Advice Centres	80	Marina contracts	66
Consumer credit	62	Marina Commission	68
County Courts	83	Marina repairs and maintenance	69
Credit	60	Marine mortgages	61
- canvassing	63	Merchantable quality	13
- liability	63	Misrepresentation	12,16,38
- licencing	62		
- outstanding payments	33	Negligence	18,22,53
- reference agencies	63		
Criminal law	7,8,9	Overdrafts	60
Damage	18	Personal loans	61

Page

Persons in trade or business	37,73
Private sellers	37,46,52
Prosecutions	75
- official	75
- private	75
Proceedings	86
- court offices	86
- cross examination	88
- costs	86,88
- names of respondents	84
- out of court settlements	77
- pre-trial reviews	86
- commencement	86
Publicity	53
Reasonable judgements	23
Regulations	8
Retailers	11,78
SBBNF	20,22,29
Second hand goods	12,37
Second mortgages	61
Services	17,50,55
Short weight or measure	9,74
Sole agencies	52
Solicitors	80,84
Stolen property	44
Suits	8
Summons	84,86
Surveys	55
- defects	55
- costs	56
Uncollected goods	25
VAT	30
Viewing	52
Witnesses	76,87
YBDSA	49